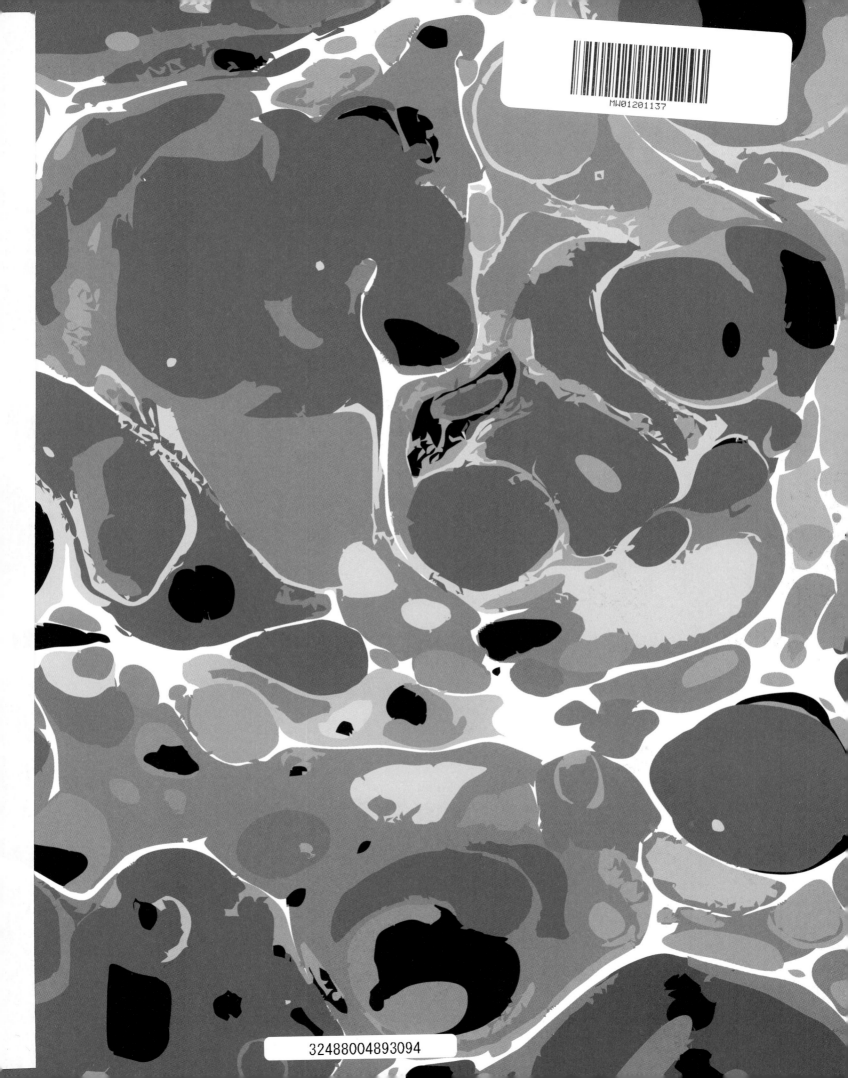

MW01201137

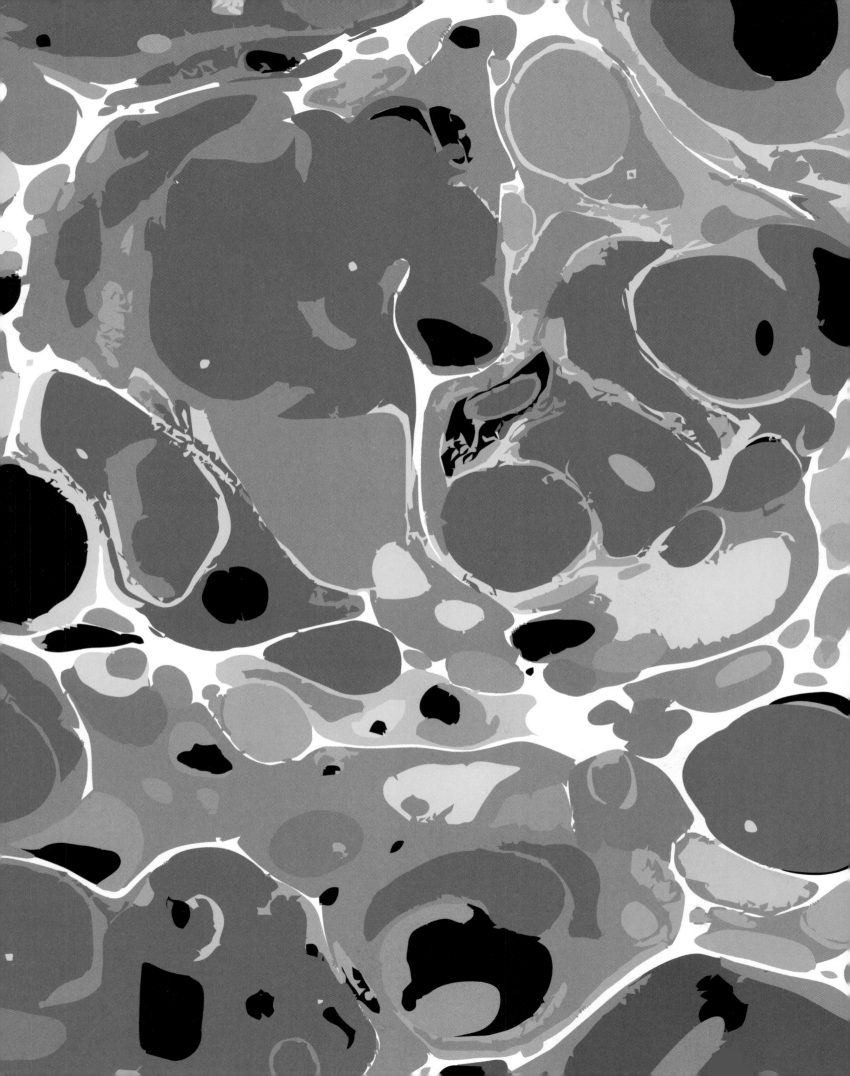

THE
PATTERNED
INTERIOR

THE PATTERNED INTERIOR
GREG NATALE

FOREWORD BY MARTYN LAWRENCE BULLARD
PHOTOGRAPHY BY ANSON SMART

New York · Paris · London · Milan

I dedicate this book to my father,
who passed away during its production.
My creative side was something my
father always encouraged, and it was thanks
to that encouragement, his love and the
example of his own hard work ethic that
I was inspired to follow my vocation in
design with passion and tenacity.

FRANCESCO NATALE

August 9, 1925 – August 18, 2017

CONTENTS

FOREWORD

by Martyn Lawrence Bullard

An Australian lady I met recently at a Paris furniture fair said to me that "design was a decade behind" in her country, to which I replied, "Well then, you have obviously never seen the work of Greg Natale!" In fact, I believe Australia has an exciting, thriving, and very passionate interior design world—at the center of which, and leading the pack, is Greg. His fearless designs, passion for color and pattern, and sense of modern glamour are in a class of their own. This new book perfectly exemplifies Greg's talents. It shows his broad range and worldly design sense, which he customizes to each client and their projects, yet always with a beautiful and cohesive signature that is purely and totally his own.

Greg's inspirations are gathered from historical references to every period and put together in a modern and sexy way. A comfort level that oozes luxury yet retains the casualness modern day living demands. I am particularly fond of his layering, a difficult skill to master, with which he brings personality to each space; whether eclectic or minimal, Greg manages to give each project its own look, while maintaining his own design language.

With twelve exceptional interiors in this tome, we get to see Greg's full spectrum of talents, highlighting his ability to shift between styles and periods, but always maintaining spaces that feel exciting and fresh. He perfectly curates and executes his interiors with signature panache.

I especially love seeing the power of pattern in Greg's work. He demonstrates the use of fabrics, wall coverings, tiles, and rugs in bold designs that are singularly wonderful, yet fearlessly mixed and matched in the way only he knows how. He makes his spaces sing in unison magnificently.

Greg proves himself in this book to be not just a leader in the field in his own country, but to be a world-class tastemaker. His singular style has become admired internationally, inspiring many to be true to themselves, to be more adventurous with pattern, and to live life to the fullest through fun and totally fabulous design. This is undeniably the signature of a master designer, the signature of Greg Natale.

OPPOSITE: A sculpture by Mathias Kiss presents a striking explosion of angles, continuing the metallics of the table below. In this country house in Victoria, Australia, pattern comes in many forms. Black timber paneling on the walls and parquetry floors provide an intricate study in line and a sophisticated backdrop to the artwork, table and accessories.

INTRODUCTION

In my work as an interior designer, I receive a wide range of feedback on a regular basis. Some people love a look on sight, others take a little more convincing. But it's not every day that I see a letter from an Australian icon that demonstrates to such a dramatic degree the impact of my work.

Dear Mr Natale,

I have been sent a computer-generated picture illustrating your plans for the redecoration of my hallway. I do not suffer from epilepsy but I have close friends who do. They will now be unable to visit me since the carpet you propose to use, with its pattern, will certainly trigger a fit. Are you sure the insurance will cover the medical claims against the building? Why was I not consulted???

With very real concern and best wishes,

Barry Humphries

This note from the legendary Mr Humphries, comedian, satirist and artist, best known for his alter ego Dame Edna Everage, certainly offered some feisty, albeit witty, feedback. Humor aside, it highlighted for me the power that pattern has to get people talking.

In the world of interior design, pattern is a conversation-starter. It can delight and surprise, refresh or rebel; it can shock, overwhelm, polarize or please. No two people will feel the same way about a pattern.

But more importantly, pattern can bring a space to life. It introduces a vital layer to the design of a house, delivering a dynamic buzz, adding contrast and balance, injecting warmth, detail and interest. And I couldn't live without it.

The Tailored Interior, my first book in 2014, was born from a desire to offer an insight into my design approach. Through beautiful photographs and some personal anecdotes and advice, I wanted to show that creating your own space needn't be too daunting if you apply a few simple design rules.

OPPOSITE: A stunning Andy Warhol original of rock star Mick Jagger sits above a charismatic sideboard in the Barwon River House. These two pieces set a vibrant scene for the play on pattern that follows.

While writing my first book, there were many details to which I wanted to devote more time, including treatments and textures about which there was a whole lot more to say. After all, as much as my work is about considering the big picture, it's also about curating those many important details that complete a project.

It's no secret that I relish patterned interiors. While it by no means defines all we do at Greg Natale Design, pattern is an essential part of everything we do, a signature element that we incorporate into every vignette, every space, every design. Pattern is in my DNA; I'm sure there's a patterned molecule hiding somewhere inside of me.

As with my interest in interior design, the connection with pattern began at home. My parents built their dream home in the late 1970s, which was to become my childhood home. As a teenager in an Italian immigrant household in suburban Sydney, Australia, there were several of my parents' design choices that I didn't support. I've written before about the Baroque reproduction chair I attempted to sell, and the bamboo wallpaper I took down in my teens in an effort to repaint the walls. Funnily enough, for a house that oozed late 1970s style, wallpaper wasn't the primary pattern-bearer. In our place it was all about the floors.

Patterned tiles defined the Natale family style. There were tiles in every room—the bathroom, rumpus room, formal lounge room, even the upstairs bedrooms. We had them in every color—neutrals upstairs (mainly ivory and dark brown), blue in the bathroom, green in the kitchen, with green laminate cabinetry to match.

Needless to say, at the time I thought I knew all there was to know about style, and I had an inherent dislike for those tiles. Fortunately, for my long-suffering parents, tiles are not that easy to rip up or sell. Thankfully, too, their house today, post-renovation, still features the tiles upstairs—and of course now I see how striking and wonderful they look. The irony doesn't escape me that I've since released successful collections of patterned tiles, including a range for Italian powerhouse Bisazza, and designed one or two green kitchens.

The prominence of patterned tiles in my family's house was a reflection partly of the era and partly of our Italian heritage. Italians love a tile. While I was busy railing against my parents' choice, the Italian architect, industrial designer and furniture designer Gio Ponti had been setting the bar for the use of pattern for decades.

Ponti's Parco dei Principi hotel in Sorrento, Italy, opened in 1962, incorporated thirty patterns of 20cm x 20cm ceramic tiles in a blue and white palette. The ingenuity and versatility of his bespoke

OPPOSITE: A picture in pattern: floor tiles in my parents' 1970s house in suburban Sydney, with some more pattern featured on much-loved pieces of furniture. My passion for pattern began here.

tiles are still dazzling to behold and remain one of the achievements that mark Ponti as the pioneer of contemporary pattern.

Starting my own business in 2001, eager to steer away from the minimalist white boxes that had dominated interior design in recent years, I wanted to learn more about the patterns, prints and textures that had made up such a big part of my childhood. Along with Ponti's work, I discovered two other greats, the late English designer David Nightingale Hicks and Danish designer Verner Panton. These three designers created an entirely new language for pattern in interior design, and they remain significant influences on my aesthetic today.

One of the most intriguing things about pattern is its ability to elicit a response and act as provocateur. My first project was a statement steeped in pattern. Using as a starting point the wallpaper print Steps III by Florence Broadhurst (an Australian pattern pioneer), I installed a custom-colored version of it wall-to-wall and layered it with matching linen and artwork, offsetting the pattern with blocks of dark neutrals for balance.

That project earned me my first major design award and, more interestingly, it got people talking. Controversial to some, timely to others, the project unintentionally carved out opportunities for a new Australian interior—one that was unafraid of the big notes, unapologetic and, though bold in its approach, was considered, deliberate and measured.

To this day, Greg Natale Design plays keenly in this space—although not always to the same extent. If pattern is one pillar at the core of my work, then the two others are tailoring (a careful curating and editing of every space) and layering (a considered building up of those key elements—walls, floors, furniture, soft furnishings and accessories—that make a space warm and welcoming). For me, the most appealing use of pattern in interiors comes from respecting the role it plays in layering and tailoring within a space.

With this book, I share my love of pattern and reveal the many impressive ways in which it can be used to enliven, enhance and create environments. I'll share with you a range of projects that illustrate the impact pattern has on a space. The inspiring photographs of homes I've designed and the accompanying stories about them are laid out to reveal the world of possibilities that pattern can offer, no matter if your preference is for an all-out effect or a more subtle statement.

Pattern provokes, it unites, it inspires and it gets us talking. It is my sincere hope that this book will ignite (or rekindle) in you a passion for pattern . . . and perhaps it might just start a conversation.

OPPOSITE: That provocative carpet, offset by wallpaper in a white-on-white chevron pattern. When I designed this hallway for a Sydney apartment block, I had no idea of the controversy it would spark.

A GRAND ENTRANCE *reflects* SPANISH ORIGINS

The quiet, leafy suburbs of western Sydney are the last place you'd expect to find a hint of Hollywood, yet this sprawling residence contains one undoubtedly theatrical element within its walls. My clients, a couple with two children, had fallen in love with the type of double staircase favored by Southern belles, soap stars and certain celebrities, and they asked me to create one for their family home.

Never one to shy away from a bold design gesture, I was only too happy to accommodate their request. After all, nothing says "grand entrance" quite like a staircase, and a double staircase makes twice as much of a statement. I could foresee the opportunities of incorporating pattern at both an architectural and decorative level, and that was before I even started on the rest of the house.

The other two key components of my clients' brief were a strong Mediterranean influence and a predominantly white and black palette. Together with the staircase, these led me to consider the Spanish Revival style so popular in the Hollywood Hills and Los Angeles. And so began a design that incorporated some of the wonderful elements of Spanish Revival architecture, such as a white stucco exterior, terra-cotta roofs, repeated arches, patterned tiles and iron details. On the staircase itself and throughout this three-story, five-bedroom house, pattern is evident at every level—in the very fabric of the building, its lines and interior architecture, as well as in the applied finishes and decorative treatments.

The staircase is one of a few design elements that combine to deliver maximum impact as you enter. From the pillared porte cochère, a pair of huge black iron doors marks the transition from exterior to interior. Their pattern shows a delicacy that belies their size and draws warmth from the terra-cotta floor tiles, offering the first of a series of spaces that heighten the sense of arrival. Following these, a large arched door with black timber paneling opens into the main reception area. That arch takes its cue from the smaller motifs of the iron doors and introduces a story of curves that gains momentum through the house.

Vast, open and filled with light, the reception area features an abundance of white due to its walls and marble floors. But it is the black details that define this zone, and the double staircase plays a major role here. The slender lines of the iron balustrade, repeated on the floor above, provide an appealing feature that is reinforced by the lines of black paint along the chair rails, cornices and on the ceiling. At the next layer of décor, the wall lamp bases and picture frames combine with the rings of the pendant light, rug and entrance table below to create a study in lines and circles that gives this space its strength and character.

PREVIOUS PAGE: Monochrome patterned tiles give a dramatic flair to the impressive staircase of this grand Sydney home. The tiles are one of the elements of Spanish Revival style that is featured throughout the residence and give it its character.

OPPOSITE: Huge black iron doors, followed by a large arched door with black timber paneling, are part of a series of entrance spaces that enhance the sense of arrival. The intricate detail of the iron doors, thrown into dramatic relief by the terra-cotta tiles below, is a hint of the dramatic elements to come.

For the stairs themselves, I drew on a common attribute of Spanish Revival design by choosing patterned tiles for the risers. Here, I alternated three different monochrome patterns, balancing that visual highlight with black granite treads. Against the white of the walls, ceilings and marble floor, the dialogue between pattern and solid black brings a sense of drama to the space.

From that grand entrance, the living areas continue the use of black lines to highlight and frame the white surfaces. In these rooms, I introduced a chair rail to break up the expanse of wall space, defining it with a black line for consistency and using navy blue patterned wallpaper for the lower section. This rich blue of the wallpaper, which runs through the family room, kitchen, dining area, bedrooms and study, provides an essential pop of color against the monochromes, while its small squares add interest. Intense blues also feature in furniture and accessories throughout, balanced by neutral silver and brightened by occasional bursts of terra-cotta, a reminder of the house's colorful roofs.

Generous square panels on the ceilings of the living areas reference the grids of the wallpaper on a larger plane, while certain pieces of furniture lend their own structure to the play on pattern. In the bedrooms, silver and blue furnishings add color to the white walls and ceilings and black-painted moldings. Given the build-up of layers in these smaller spaces, the mood here is softer and more intimate, its effect enhanced by the addition of charcoal and white carpet in a pattern reminiscent of filigree work. In the bathrooms, the monochromes enjoy another dramatic moment via cement floor tiles in a graceful Mediterranean style. Against these, white subway wall tiles keep the room light and bright, allowing the floor treatment to remain the star.

It is outside, in a pair of interconnecting loggias spanning the length of the house, where the patterns of architectural and decorative elements come together in another grand statement. The repeated arches of the white-painted colonnade form an elegant line that emphasizes the house's hacienda-inspired design, particularly when framed by the terra-cotta roofs above and paving below. The painted exposed beams create a stunning series of lines that is echoed in the black and white striped curtains clustered softly at each pillar. Against this backdrop, the bold patterns of soft furnishings and the blue of the pool come into focus, a stylistic bridge between the interior and exterior palettes.

From its impressive series of entrances to its lavish rear exterior, this home showcases how the power of pattern and line can make an impact simultaneously at the large scale and the small, culminating in something at once theatrical and inviting.

OPPOSITE: Looking back at the arched entrance from beneath the staircases, a study in line and balance is evident, where circles in the pendant light, console table and rug offset all the angles. The bold monochrome design gives the setting added impact.

A touch of Hollywood theatrics in
the Sydney suburbs: the alternating
patterned tiles of the stair risers give an
alluring rhythm to the staircase, drawing
you upwards. The repeated lines of
the iron balustrade contribute to the
dramatic effect.

OPPOSITE: A dazzling pendant light becomes a major component of the formal dining setting, where the angled black chair backs visually link to the house's black molding. *ABOVE:* In the informal dining setting, the ceiling panels are echoed in the lines of the furniture legs. *FOLLOWING PAGES, LEFT:* Blue linen armchairs echo the hues of my Astoria wallpaper and a painting by Scott Petrie in the living room. *FOLLOWING PAGES, RIGHT:* The same wallpaper, underneath a black chair rail, runs through the main living areas, where hues of blue, gray and terra-cotta give depth and balance.

OPPOSITE: Silvery-gray furnishings give a touch of opulence to the master bedroom, with accessories adding the same vivid punches of blue that appear throughout the house. *ABOVE:* The walk-in wardrobe, which features the same charcoal and white carpet in a filigree-like pattern, balances the long line of paneling with the arcs of the seats and round light—another shared feature that links both spaces.

ABOVE: Another bedroom introduces more tones of blue, with a few red touches that link to the terra-cotta that features so prominently outside. *OPPOSITE: M*onochromes define this bathroom, but their treatment via different patterns and finishes ensures variety, with the Mediterranean-style tiles bringing a delicate flourish. *FOLLOWING PAGES, LEFT AND RIGHT:* The interconnecting loggias, with their repeated arches, black stripes and beams, and bright terra-cotta tiles, showcase the hacienda style that is central to this house's design.

NATURE *as* MUSE *with* *a* TROPIC MODERN TWIST

When I'm considering how to incorporate pattern and color into an interior design, inspiration presents itself in many ways. Sometimes the era of a house will suggest the type of lines I'll use; other times the client–designer collaborative process will unearth a certain mood or palette that sparks my creative direction. And occasionally something as simple and beautiful as a house's natural surroundings proves the strongest inspiration of all.

This was certainly the case with one client's extraordinary Hamilton Island villa on Australia's Great Barrier Reef. One of the beautiful Whitsunday Islands off the Queensland coast, Hamilton is home to stunning native bushland, pristine beaches and world-famous coral reefs. It was the colors, shapes and textures of this unique natural setting that I wanted to weave into the interior design.

In a place synonymous with luxury tourism, there is something of the resort style about this eight-bedroom residence. It's not surprising, really—captivated by the beauty of the neighboring multi-award-winning resort, my client charmed its architect out of retirement for the design of his own resort-style villa. And while this is undoubtedly an exceptional vacation home for a young family, one of the features it shares with Australian resort living is a focus on bringing the outdoors in. The house enjoys exquisite views of the Coral Sea through the native hoop pines, as well as abundant plant life at its doors, so establishing a connection to those elements was central to the design.

A delightfully open plan means the villa comprises a series of interconnected pavilions that flow on to courtyards, lawns, pools and secluded coastal lookouts. At every turn, tree trunks, leaves and water are not only visible but also accessible, and it was my job to emphasize that accessibility through the use of pattern and color.

Timber is a highlight of the house's design and New Guinea Rosewood has been used throughout, its rich tones setting the scene for the layers that follow. Timber panels bring their own inherent patterns to the interior, their intricate lines and burls adorning boardwalks and floors, walls and ceilings, louvered windows and doors.

Against the timber backdrop, I introduced a palette centered on olive green and blush, glorious reminders of the native flora, fauna and reefscape beyond, and a way of inviting their beauty indoors. The main living room illustrates this blend perfectly—a generous sofa setting covered in a print of olive-green Monstera leaves seems to emerge from the plant-filled courtyard behind. Its effect is heightened by surrounding indoor plants, with an eclectic assortment of walnut timber tables

PREVIOUS PAGE: The Monstera leaf print of a sofa brings a touch of the tropics to the neutral tones of the side tables and rug in this villa on Australia's Hamilton Island. The furnishings throughout connect the place's design to its beautiful natural surroundings.

OPPOSITE: Rosewood timber is a prominent feature of the villa, its long lines bringing their own pattern to the design. Boardwalks such as this one at the entrance connect many of the spaces, ensuring an open flow between areas.

contributing darker tones to the mix. Patterned cushions in shades of pink, gray and green add detail and reflect the warmth of the timber. Balancing this are the neutral gray tones of a pair of patterned armchairs upholstered in a mottled fabric and an oversized marble slab-effect rug.

This distinctive combination ripples throughout each of the house's open living spaces. In the dining setting, contemporary chairs in gray leather and textured green fabric are paired with a vast timber table, while the dappled patterning of a rug below recalls the familiar palette of blush, olive, black and white. The fine lines of a pair of timber pendant lights finish the picture. Across the lush courtyard, hanging glass lamps wrapped in twine preside over the garden terrace, a perennially open space with a stylistic connection to the plants beyond. Here, green and timber seating picks up the hues of the rug, while the vaulted timber ceiling and stone wall provide their own study in texture and line.

Led by the details of timber, stone and plant life, pattern takes many forms throughout the house, from organic leaf prints to shell-like furrows to looser abstract shapes. The effect is that of a tropical paradise with a warm but modern edge, where the link between inside and out is always evident.

Even the master bedroom picks up the theme, taking the softer blush tones of the Great Barrier Reef's precious coral as its core color. In this hue, cushions with a pattern like shattered stone, as well as a throw and accessories, display a softer take on the rosewood of the wardrobe doors and floor, while gray bed furnishings in a banana leaf pattern maintain another link with the lush tropical surrounds.

The terraces and cabanas around the house's two pools perhaps best unite setting and style, the natural and the nuanced. Flanking an infinity pool set on the same level as the house's entrance, one terrace features green Monstera-print chairs, a green rug and timber furniture that speak eloquently to the treetops outside. Opposite, sun loungers in neutral tones echo the cool gray roofs and stone wall behind, warmed by the rosy hues of the cushions and timber decking.

Two stories below, those same colors come together in a large pavilion by the second pool and a series of cabanas arranged before it. Timber, stone, green furnishings and neutrals absorb and reflect the hues of the environment, while the coral-toned sun loungers, arrayed like sea treasures themselves, recall the reef beyond.

Looking out to the sea, sky and tree life, and back towards the villa with its organic patterns and hues, the link between outdoors and in reverberates. Every scene reflects the images of the surrounding that inspired it. Nature, here, is both the frame and the picture.

OPPOSITE: The greens and timber of the upstairs pool terrace establish a serene connection with the pines and bushland outside, with a rusted steel wall sculpture by Dan Lorrimer adding another layer of texture to the timber walls.

OPPOSITE: The dining area showcases the villa's open-plan design. Here, the green fabric of the dining chairs and the timber table continue the tones of the plants beyond. My Vapour rug brings together the house's central palette of olive green and blush. *ABOVE:* In the main living area, a Minotti sofa covered in a Monstera leaf print echoes the plant forms in the courtyard behind. *FOLLOWING PAGES:* Another view of the same room reveals the sofa in its entirety, offset by blush-toned cushions, armchairs by Kelly Wearstler and my gray Fragment rug.

ABOVE: In the garden terrace, planes of green in the Minotti seating pick up the hue from the Porter Teleo rug. A powder-coated steel sculpture by Hannah Quinlivan and a bronze and travertine coffee table introduce new materials against the backdrop of timber and stone.
OPPOSITE: A setting of poolside sun loungers in neutral tones gains warmth from the blush cushions and timber decking, enhanced by another rusted steel wall sculpture by Dan Lorrimer.

PREVIOUS PAGES, LEFT AND RIGHT: Blush tones bring a softening touch to the master bedroom, appearing in the cushions, throws, ceramics and armchair and echoed by the neutral-hued sheer curtains. The subtle gray banana leaf print of the bed furnishings continues the link with the abundant plant life. ABOVE: Warm tones and greens link this poolside pavilion to its surroundings. OPPOSITE: The house's palette continues in the outdoor furniture.

Below the house's entrance and top floor, a series of cabanas looks out to the long stretch of lawn that leads to the large pool beyond. Against the surrounding trees and island vista, green and blush furnishings team with cool gray roofs and warm timber to reinforce the connection between indoor and outdoor living.

BOLD STATEMENTS *for* COUNTRY GLAMOUR

From one of the seductive black timber walls of a magnificent country house in Victoria, Australia, a particular portrait commands attention. The subject it depicts is not a horse or hound, as you might expect from a sprawling rural estate, nor is it a solemn ancestor surveying his domain. Here, pouting, proud and perennially sexy, is Mick Jagger—an original artwork by Andy Warhol. It is the picture of an icon captured by an icon, but it is something much more. Presiding over one of the stunning rooms in this residence, the rock star's image encapsulates the house's bold design.

Grand country estates allow for grand statements, and one of the most exhilarating challenges for an interior designer is the opportunity to work on such a large scale. With not just one vast canvas, but also several smaller ones, you have the chance to play with proportion, to try different treatments across different spaces and to inject elements of surprise throughout. All the while, you must interweave and interrelate the separate spaces, ensuring powerful, emotive connections throughout.

The owners of this two-story, five-bedroom home wanted a warm, luxe, generous residence that would nurture and delight their growing family. The building is part of a huge property that includes a horse stud, and equine elements make their way into the design at unexpected moments. For this family, comfort means plenty of texture, rich tonal variations as opposed to stark contrasts, an abundance of well-stocked bookshelves and some treasured pieces and artworks. With a palette that centered on black-stained timber and brass accents, I built up a sumptuously layered interior that features pattern at every level.

The story of pattern began with the sophisticated lines of black-stained spotted gum on the house's exterior, each panel wire-brushed to reveal its grain. Working from the outside in, I used that same timber in the entrance, seamlessly linking exterior and interior and setting the scene for what would be revealed throughout the rest of the house.

Addressing the vast expanses of wall, I elected for paneling in black-stained American oak, a striking way of introducing pattern into the structure of the house while celebrating the material itself. These panels align cleanly with the steel framework of the windows, tying the two together in a precise, bold grid. For the floors, using the same material, I looked to the French tradition of parquetry for inspiration. This handsome pattern stands alone aesthetically, contributing an extra decorative layer and a heightened level of detail throughout.

Sophistication is all very well, but I also wanted the home to exude a sexiness, something surprising and a little beguiling given its country setting. To achieve this, I introduced two elegant materials

PREVIOUS PAGE: A detail from the bar of this country house in Victoria, where the geometrics of my Diane carpet contrast with the curved furniture.

OPPOSITE: The house forms a striking silhouette against the landscape. Its exterior of black-stained spotted gum and grid of steel-framed windows provided me with inspiration for some of the interior treatments.

that I love to work with. Warm and sleek all at once, Macassar Ebony timber, with its walnut and black tones and gloss finish, plays its part in breaking up the oak and brings a special sheen to the ceilings in several areas of the house. Contrasting it, highlighting it, holding its own beautifully beside it, is gleaming brass, a strong recurring detail.

This opulent pairing enriches the master bedroom and the bar, two rooms unalike in function yet connected in form. Both feature ebony ceilings with brass inlays in a grid pattern that recalls the Shaker-style paneling of the walls. In the bedroom, the brass trim continues in the bookshelves, the walk-in-wardrobe and the dramatic master en suite bathroom, where organic black and gold marble soften its effect.

In the bar, the brass accents are echoed in more shelves and converge dramatically in the spectacular bar itself. Both rooms feature the same gray carpet of asymmetrical geometrics, which plays with the rhythm of patterns on a more muted level while providing another connection between the spaces. Similarities aside, both spaces exhibit their own individual character.

If you can't make an indulgent statement in a bedroom, where can you? To add an element of surprise to the master bedroom, I created a geometric feature wall using panels of charcoal and champagne leather. Textural, tonal and decadent, it brings together the room's palette and patterns in one grand gesture that evokes the mood of a refined retreat.

In another corner of the estate the bar shares similar lines, yet here I injected a vibrant hit of color to change the pace. The magenta in the sofa and sideboard takes its cue from that captivating Mick Jagger artwork by Andy Warhol and sends a more playful message—here, recreation, not rest, is the order of the day.

Patterns unite and uplift this house, but it is their various treatments and color pairings that really define each of the diverse spaces. The works of art featured throughout have much to do with this. When working with patterns across a grand house, it is essential that color be addressed to link the place cohesively and bind together its various aesthetic gestures with at least one commonality. To achieve this, differently purposed rooms reveal different palette combinations. The living and dining areas incorporate vibrant shades of green amid their blend of brass, blacks and grays. The sharp arcs of green in the living-room rug, the blocks of color in the leather dining chairs and the abstract patterns of the sofa cushions all create a connection that links this space to the nearby loggia and the landscaped grounds beyond.

Two contemplative spaces—the anteroom and the library—boast vivid blue seating, inspired by the tones of two paintings: one

by Australian artist Dale Frank, the other by Russian artist Anna Berezovskaya. The blue armchairs in the anteroom seem to emerge seamlessly from the blue and purple rug on which they rest. In the library, a semicircular blue velvet sofa with matching ottomans and armchairs presents an inviting setting. Both spaces also feature molded ceilings, a detail that enhances the rooms' appeal but has a greater significance. In the context of the overall design narrative, it is a major design feature, and takes me to one of my favorite spaces in the house.

At the foot of the spiraling staircase, there is a mesmerizing vignette that sums up the story of pattern in this residence. Along the floor, spanning two major wings of the house, is a lengthy rug, one of my designs, featuring a super-sized version of a chain link pattern. Above, the molded ceiling directly mirrors the pattern and layout of the rug. Decorative ceilings were always a must for the design of this house, but I wanted to take it further by reflecting ceilings and floors to make the ultimate statement of cohesion and connection. From the moment you enter the house, it becomes an all-encompassing design language that immerses as it delights, overhead and underfoot.

There is something so luxurious, cocooning and transportive about a space where the ceiling mirrors the floor. The two patterned parts make a whole, enclosing you in its harmony and allowing you to feel at one with the space. In a large house such as this, it also becomes a smart device that brings the two elements closer, making the entire area warmer, more human in scale and cohesive.

That same chain link pattern appears in smaller versions in other spaces, creating a strong connection between different rooms in the house. The anteroom reveals the same mirroring technique using another pattern, as its black ceiling beams reflect the irregular lines of a vibrant rug on the floor. While the ceiling pattern is different here, what the anteroom shares with the main hallway is the marble-effect wallpaper on the ceiling between the moldings. Its look is soft, almost textural, an example of pattern functioning at a more subtle level and another connection between the spaces.

Standing in that magical spot before the staircase, enfolded by pattern above and below, the spirit of the house is manifest. Set against the black-stained, timber-paneled walls and floor, the ribbon stairs beckon you inside the family's dream home. The soft geometrics of the rug, the intricate bespoke brass balustrade and the luscious ebony finish all promise luxurious comforts to come, in a sexy, sophisticated haven that's a little bit country, a little bit rock 'n' roll, and that celebrates the power of pattern.

OPPOSITE: Ceiling mirrors floor along the lengthy hallway, with an enlarged chain link pattern featured on both. Looking back to the entrance, the cocooning effect of the pattern is flanked by eye-catching works of art. To the left, a painting by Australian abstract artist Dale Frank provides a burst of color; to the right, a sculpture by local artist Dion Horstmans picks up the metallics that are such an integral part of the interior design.

FOLLOWING PAGES, LEFT: A blue velvet sofa in the library echoes the curves of the molded ceiling and is set off dramatically by the French-style design of the timber floors. Delicate gold lace curtains introduce pattern at a softer, textural level, the perfect backdrop for the stunning pendant light. *FOLLOWING PAGES, RIGHT:* At the base of the brass and ebony ribbon staircase, a play on lines takes place. Sun flows in through the sheer curtains, highlighting the various metallic surfaces and the steel framework of the windows, which is in turn mirrored in the timber panels. Above the oak parquetry, a brass and walnut table and another sculpture by Dion Horstmans echo the metallics of the balustrade.

PREVIOUS PAGES: Providing a tonal link to the outdoors, bursts of green invigorate the light-filled living and dining areas, in the arcs of the rug, in blocks of color on the dining chairs and in abstract flourishes on the cushions. Against this, a range of grays, blacks and metallics complete the palette, with geometrics, grids, long lines and indulgent curves combining for a richly patterned mélange. *OPPOSITE:* A different view of the living room, where a bronze Richard Blackwell sculpture above the fireplace breaks up the grid effect of the bookshelves. *ABOVE:* In another entrance to the house, the curves of a brass sculpture and vintage Murano glass and brass lamp bases combine with the unusual angles of the mirror and long line of custom-built shelf for a dramatic result. Pattern is integrated into every level of this house.

Bookshelves were a must for the owners, together with rich tonal variations and plenty of texture throughout. Here, an attractive brass and ebony bookshelf acts as a divider between the living room (front) and anteroom (behind), where the vivid blues of a Dale Frank painting are beautifully displayed. As well as showcasing personal treasures, its structure adds a delightfully complex layer to the rooms.

OPPOSITE: The armchairs in the anteroom were inspired by the tones of Dale Frank's painting. Here, the ceiling panels mirror the intersecting angles of the colorful rug below, with the same marble-effect wallpaper on the ceiling that features in the main hallway. *ABOVE:* The brass legs of a console table in the hallway provide a delicate study in line beneath a vintage Murano glass mirror.

PREVIOUS PAGES: In the bar, where the magenta sofa commands attention and demands fun, coffered ceilings with brass inlays converge in the standout bar itself. OPPOSITE: In a breakout space in the bar, the curtains provide a subtle pattern and abstract texture against the stronger lines of the furniture. A bold pendant light by Holly Hunt delivers the finishing touch. ABOVE: Andy Warhol's portrait of Mick Jagger was the inspiration for the bold palette of this room. The lavish faceted sideboard takes its cue from the sofa nearby.

ABOVE: Brass-lined doors and shelves work with the timber-paneled ceiling and floor to bring elegant, gleaming lines to the cellar. OPPOSITE: Mosaic tiles in a chain link pattern and a mirrored ceiling bestow an all-encompassing glamorous touch to the bar's powder room. FOLLOWING PAGES: A feature wall of charcoal and champagne leather panels makes a grand and glorious statement that spans the length of the master bedroom and presents a softer tonal pairing beneath the striking ebony and brass ceiling.

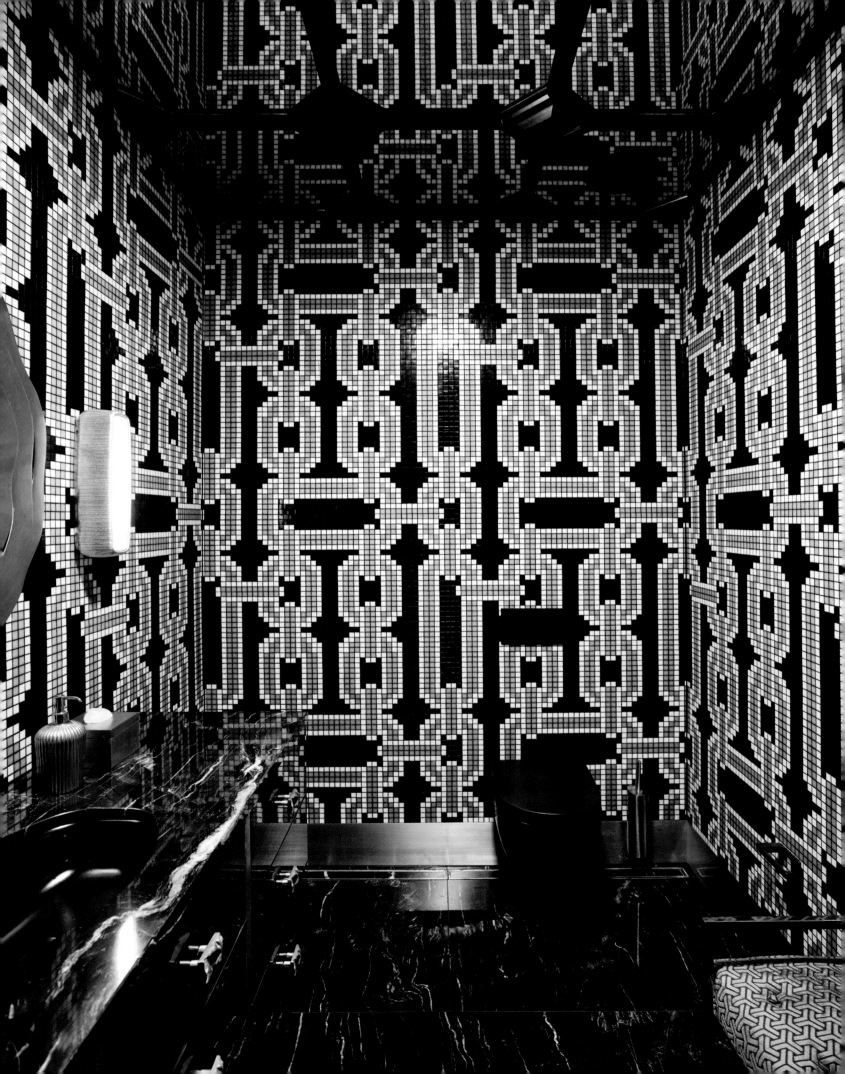

OPPOSITE: Velvet armchairs in a blush hue echo the tones of a painting by Jo Davenport at a soft, textural level and temper the finishes of black, brass and gray. ABOVE: Another bedroom vignette: a bold abstract work by Waldemar Kolbusz offers a pop of color behind two vintage Pierre Cardin lamps. FOLLOWING PAGES, LEFT: Metallic tiles and a gold-leaf mirror add their moody sheen to the ebony vanity in one powder room. FOLLOWING PAGES, RIGHT: The custom-designed bath offers strong lines that anchor the play of brass and black marble in the master en suite bathroom.

OPPOSITE AND ABOVE: Adjacent to the remarkable master bedroom, the expansive walk-in wardrobe echoes its ceiling patterns and geometric carpet. The addition of a circular skylight is highlighted by two charming dome-shaped lamps. *FOLLOWING PAGES:* Bookshelves offer a chance for splashes of color in one of the children's bedrooms, with playful logos and letters injecting fun into the black and gold palette.

PREVIOUS PAGES, LEFT AND RIGHT: Geometrics in the rug and tiled floor, panels on the timber walls and benches, a marble backsplash ... the indoor/outdoor spaces sing with pattern, while verdant plants establish a connection between the areas. ABOVE: Timber paneling and chevron flooring give textural detail to the gym. OPPOSITE: A bolt of blue amid the monochromes, the pool features its own play on pattern. FOLLOWING PAGES: The house's exterior takes on different aspects in the shifting light.

A MIDTOWN JEWEL BOX REVEALS *its* TREASURES

New York. So many people have written about it, sung about it, photographed it, filmed it and celebrated it that for me to have the opportunity to design an apartment here was a dream come true. It is a fitting place for dreams, after all. Alicia Keys sings of a concrete jungle, a place dreams are made of, in "Empire State of Mind." Chip away at the surface of that concrete jungle and a world of color and creativity exists, with so many of the city's buildings giving no hint of the treasures that lie within. My clients' apartment is one of these, situated in a fairly nondescript building in Midtown Manhattan. Like a jewel box, it reveals its close-kept wonders only once you enter its front door.

The sophisticated tones of navy blue are one of the first sights that strike you upon entering. My clients, a couple with three children, have a great fondness for the hue, particularly the blue of one of my wallpapers (appropriately named Astoria), and so this became the starting point for my design. I incorporated the wallpaper into the master bedroom, where its blue-on-blue squares bring an elegant finish, and I painted the walls of the main rooms navy to tie the palette together. Balanced by white ceilings and black-stained oak floors, the effect creates a refined backdrop for the pattern play that takes place.

Pattern is a key factor of the furnishings in this apartment, but it also plays another role beyond the decorative—here, it becomes a useful tool in tackling issues of limited space. At just under eight feet, the ceilings of this post-war apartment are quite low, and with no crown moldings and only beams visible, the original space looked cramped and lacking in definition. In addressing the interior architecture, I used paint and pattern to visually transform the walls and ceilings, the result of which is best observed in the design of the living room.

Here, I created a new, higher ceiling zone by installing crown moldings above the low beams and painting these and the skirting boards white. Between these, I painted the walls, including the low beams, navy, resulting in a tailored, crisp look where those beams seem to disappear into the walls. I also broke up the ceiling space by adding two faux beams, the long lines of which visually suggest a larger area. On the ceiling panels between the beams, I incorporated wallpaper in a black and white malachite pattern, adding a layer of detail that softly frames the room without visually reducing its proportions. Below, that pattern is complemented by a blue and white snakeskin-style rug by fashion designer Diane von Furstenberg. The organic lines of both surfaces contrast with the bold geometrics of the artworks on the wall and the striking pieces of furniture.

PREVIOUS PAGE: A vintage side table by Paul Evans is one of many stunning metallic pieces in this New York apartment. Its brass and chrome blocks maintain a warm glow against the palette of navy blue and white.

OPPOSITE: A remarkable vintage console table of brass and glass makes a strong statement at the entrance. The varying lines of its unusual legs work with the curves of the lamp base and round mirror above to create a setting that is all about glamour.

The fashion legend is one of several style icons whose pieces I selected for the apartment. New York is a city of icons, and I find it fitting that this apartment incorporates pieces from some of my favorite designers, present and past. In the living room, a freestanding bar in a champagne-hued metallic from the Florence Broadhurst Collection displays a design by the late Australian doyenne of pattern that almost makes it a piece of art. Vintage Paul Evans side tables continue the emphasis on metallics, with a luxe blue sofa by Kelly Wearstler and white chairs by Cassina providing inviting links to the central palette.

Vintage pieces are one of the highlights of the apartment, as are metallics, with brass and gold bringing a bold glow to the polished setting. A vintage console table at the entrance, its brass legs reminiscent of organ pipes, makes a unique statement that sets the tone for the rest of the home. With the sultry curves of a brass-based lamp and a circular mirror above it, the vignette evokes the spirit of another world, one of martinis, jazz music and moody lighting. Here, the use of pattern is considered and controlled, with special pieces making their mark, the chic palette enveloping the space, and a variety of rugs delivering much of the detail, warmth and intimacy.

In the dining room, around the honey-gold burl veneer of a table by Jonathan Adler, brass vintage chairs and a light by Gaetano Sciolari present a handsome picture of stylized lines, offset by the sharp, round geometrics of a blue, gray and white rug. In the bedrooms, patterned wallpaper enriches the scheme of navy walls, taking on different finishes in the changing light. The master bedroom features the square-patterned wallpaper; the children's bedroom displays another of my wallpaper designs in a loose dot print. Soft furnishings add bursts of varied pattern and color, reinforcing the blues and reinterpreting the golds in a softer layer, while the different shapes in the rugs bring vitality. Every room, every space offers precious pieces that surprise and delight, with an unusually shaped mirror framed in pink metallic presiding over the master bedroom, and mesmerizing vintage brass and chrome artworks in the children's bedroom.

With Carnegie Hall down one block and the Plaza Hotel and Central Park two more away, this apartment is in good company among a few of the city's landmarks, despite its unprepossessing exterior. As Keys recognizes, there is something about those streets that works its magic, something about their lights that inspires you—and inspire me they did. To create a treasure trove that combines poise with poetry, that keeps to a restrained palette while introducing moments of unexpected detail, was a challenge and a pleasure. Let's hear it for New York. And pattern.

OPPOSITE: After the gray Carrara marble that marks the entrance area, the floors feature black-stained oak parquetry, which takes on dramatically different looks according to the light. The op art piece by Jorgen Peters on the wall is one of several vintage elements that adorn the apartment.

FOLLOWING PAGES: The seductive snakeskin-like pattern of a rug by Diane von Furstenberg echoes the marble look of the wallpaper on the living room ceiling, creating a soft, cocooning effect. Against this, the bold blue velvet sofa and white Cassina chairs reinforce the palette pairing of navy walls and white-painted beams and cornices. A pair of graphic prints draws together the blue and gold tones, with various cushions presenting another attractive play on pattern.

PREVIOUS PAGES, LEFT: The champagne-hued metallic bar by Florence Broadhurst reveals exquisite pattern work in its shapely doors.
PREVIOUS PAGES, RIGHT: In the dining room, brass vintage chairs and a Gaetano Sciolari light present a striking composition of line,
enhanced by the sharp curves of my London rug. Abstract paintings by Scott Petrie lend a burst of color and energy to the space.
OPPOSITE: Soft furnishings continue the play on blues in the master bedroom, with the curves and colors of my Rio rug changing the pace.
ABOVE: A vintage lamp creates its own standout lines before my Astoria wallpaper, which was the starting point for the apartment's design.

ABOVE: A side table by Tom Dixon and cabinet by Jonathan Adler combine with a couple of decorative artworks to present a collection of eclectic shapes in the children's bedroom. OPPOSITE: The palette of blue, white and gold is highlighted in standout elements such as the block patterns of my Memphis rug and the eye-catching vintage metallic artworks behind the beds.

VICTORIAN CHARM ENTERS *a* VIBRANT NEW ERA

For an interior designer, it is always an exhilarating feeling when your work has delighted and inspired a client. That thrill reaches an entirely new level when the same work delights and inspires another potential client to the point where they ask for a similar design for their own house. In my first book, *The Tailored Interior*, I featured a home that teamed white ceilings and skirting with powder-blue walls and monochrome highlights throughout. Since the book's release, I have had three requests to recreate (or at least revisit) that particular look.

What is it about this combination of elements? I believe the pairing of white paint with a pale wash of blue creates an elegant, serene backdrop for the interior design that follows. Against that ceiling and wall setting, the addition of monochromes brings sophistication; add metallic accents to that and the result speaks of bold, luxe tailoring.

This was the vision of a family of four, for whom I renovated a charming Victorian-era house in Geelong, Australia. Their four-bedroom residence is a generous, light-filled space that lends itself beautifully to such a graceful mix. The owners wanted a duck-egg shade of blue on the walls, and I introduced this color into other furnishings across a range of patterns so it would become a key component of the design.

Arches are a strong architectural feature of the house and an intrinsic part of the white and blue wall structure. Inspired by the arches of the original exterior, I painted the interior ones in white to match, so they appear as a continuation of the lines of white skirting and stand out against the blue walls. Some arches feature sculptural details, others glass paneling, but all contribute to the house's architectural lines of pattern. They seem to merge with the white paint above the picture rail, visually carving out more space and light. As a series, they give a sense of cohesion and connection to the rooms.

At a smaller, decorative level, I repeated those arches in the doors of the kitchen cabinetry and in the curves of the furniture, lamps and mirrors. Domes, arcs and circles create their own design story, resonating with the lines of the architecture and balancing the long right angles of the ceiling paneling and skirting.

In this house, pattern also provides an attractive stylistic link via the floor coverings. Throughout the hallway and bedrooms runs a black and white carpet of my design in a repeated geometric pattern. Not only does it provide a layer of warmth and detail, this carpet draws together the different rooms, linking them and adding interest and energy.

In the hallway, the alignment of the carpet's print lures you into the house and its corridor of arches, echoed by the metallic frames and

PREVIOUS PAGE: Decades of design bring pattern together in the master bedroom of a house in Geelong, Australia. A Fornasetti cushion in a classic print sits on my post-war-style Hudson chair upholstered in houndstooth, with an antique screen behind displaying a delicately moody scene.

OPPOSITE: The arches of the original exterior of this Victorian-era residence inspired my introduction of arches into both the interior architecture and décor. The renovated house is a blend of old and new elements, and one of the challenges of the design was establishing consistency across all spaces.

shapes of mirrors and works of art. In the bedrooms, the carpet provides a cocooning layer, the intricacy of which is balanced by the muted expanses of painted walls and ceilings. I kept the ceiling paneling to a minimum in these rooms, opting for a single framing line and allowing pattern and form to emerge from the different palettes and vintage-style pendant lights that feature in each room.

The black and white carpet is also present in the formal dining room and is a defining feature of the space. There are two dining areas in this house, and each responds powerfully to its particular patterned flooring. In the formal dining room, a lacquered white table and black leather-upholstered chairs extend and highlight the monochromes of the carpet, supported by a white and gilt cabinet and black-framed mirror behind. What elevates this setting are the petal-shaped brass chair backs and brass domed lamps—as well as bringing an exquisite gleam to the space, they also reference the repetition of curves in the house.

The informal dining area adjoins the kitchen, and across both these spaces the floor is covered with my geometric tiles in blue, black and white. They bring a vibrant spirit to the area, giving it all the buzz you'd expect from the hub of a family home. Here, a round white table and unique keyhole-shaped chairs offer a playful series of curves that continues to riff on the language of arches. Smaller circles in the cabinet door handles and pendant light reinforce this theme and balance the long lines of the island bench, joinery, walls and ceiling. As elsewhere, brass elements inject some glamour, even in this more relaxed space.

Those geometric tiles continue into the living area. While they are undoubtedly the stars of the kitchen, here they play more of a supporting role to the larger planes of furniture. The soft gray of the sofa and deep blue of a pair of armchairs draw on the darker tones of the tiles, with a range of cushions bringing their own splashes of color and pattern. The rich gold of two more armchairs and a patterned rug bring another layer of color, capped by the stunning pendant light above.

A tiled living area might be an unexpected choice, but it works due to the open-plan flow of the spaces and the ample layering here. It presents a fresh case for the ways in which pattern can function, and it's a technique I explored further in the floor of the main bathroom. Tiles were the obvious choice here, yet the monochrome geometrics of these tiles recall the pattern of the carpet that comes before them. It is as if one floor pattern has augmented and become another, and yet it still provides another subtle cohesive link between the spaces. This is one of the many reasons I love pattern, for its power to connect, enliven and assume a variety of roles within the theater of design.

OPPOSITE: Duck-egg blue walls, white ceilings and skirting, monochromes and metallics, arches and geometrics—this hallway vignette encapsulates the house's elegant mix.

PREVIOUS PAGES, LEFT: Curved brass chair backs and lamps in the formal dining room continue the house's metallic accents, while echoing the shape of the arches throughout. Black, white and gilt in the furniture maintain a tightly edited picture that stems from the carpet's tones. *PREVIOUS PAGES, RIGHT:* Geometric patterned floor tiles link the living space to the informal dining area and kitchen behind, where a playful dining setting, pendant lights and collection of Fornasetti plates on the wall maintain the play on rounded forms.

RIGHT: In the living room, major pieces of furniture keep the focus on the layers of gray, blue and gold, with the patterned floor tiles playing a secondary role. A painting by Jo Davenport reflects the warm tones of the rug, cushions, throw and table.

OPPOSITE: Taking their cue from the brass light, warmer tones in the artworks by Claire Bridge and the cushions balance the cool blue and monochrome mix in the master bedroom. ABOVE: The dark hues of the antique screen in one corner of the room are contrasted by the modern patterns of the chair and carpet. Panels in the cabinet and button tufting in the ottoman transform the white surfaces.

PREVIOUS PAGES, LEFT: The bold geometrics of the cushions and a painting by Zac Koukoravas bring dynamic lines to the son's bedroom. *PREVIOUS PAGES, RIGHT:* Monochrome tiles in the main bathroom recall the pattern of the carpet; a familiar look in a new format that suits its setting. *OPPOSITE:* Delicate brass elements grace the daughter's bedroom, while a print by Megan Hess picks up the monochromes of the carpet. *ABOVE:* Another Megan Hess print echoes the soft pink of the throw and stained glass window.

LAVISH GESTURES *on a* CHIC CITY SCALE

Twenty years ago, when I was embarking on my career in interior design, I had my first glimpse of The Horizon. This remarkable Australian apartment building, designed by the late Harry Seidler and completed in 1998, was already causing a stir in Sydney, the way Seidler buildings do. Forty-three stories tall, it towered over its inner-city neighbors, casting an unforgettable silhouette with its unique scalloped balconies, which were designed to gain maximum access to the sweeping city views.

I was already a fan of the modernist architect's work, and this building captured my heart. It is a masterpiece of design and a tribute to Seidler's genius; its lines so complex yet clean. I wanted in. But I was in my early twenties, just out of university, and it wasn't to be. For years to come, I'd often drive by it just to gaze and think to myself, "One day . . .".

Today, I am the proud owner of a two-bedroom apartment in The Horizon. As I look out from one of those wave-crested concrete balconies, I feel immensely honored and lucky to live in this iconic structure, which has become a part of the Sydney skyline itself.

When I had the chance to bring my own design to this space, top of my list was a predominance of light, bright tones that would maximize its generous proportions. I wanted white to feature strongly, with lots of brass and metallic touches—these would work together to harness that brilliant Sydney sunlight, then filter and feature it throughout.

To begin, I wallpapered the entire place in a light marble pattern of gold on a white background. In apartments, which are generally open-plan, wallpaper is such an effective and elegant way of tying the various spaces together and creating an impact at first sight.

Led by the wallpaper, pattern in this apartment takes on a textural presence through several elements. I wanted to have a mirrored wall in the living room that would reflect the view of the Sydney Harbour Bridge outside. Rather than plain glass, I opted for a marbled overlay, which gives it the look of aged mirror and bestows a gently burnished finish on everything it reflects. Stylistically, it echoes the marbling of the wallpaper and the top of the coffee table, allowing these organic swirls to play together at one visual level. The window treatments display another use of pattern that is textural in its effect. White sheer curtains contain a subtle chevron stripe that, from a distance, enhances the illusion of their volume, while up close revealing delicate detail. That stripe also appears in the semi-sheer roman blinds of the living room.

At a structural level, pattern plays a role in the grid effect of the mirrored wall and in the ceiling coffers, which I introduced to bring the lights into focus. The shape of those coffers is echoed below in the

PREVIOUS PAGE: In my own apartment, in inner-city Sydney, pattern comes into play via several elements. My taupe and white Yves carpet provides a geometric feature throughout, upon which the predominant tones of white and gold interact, punctuated by pops of navy. The curtains contain a subtle stripe that brings another layer of detail to the space.

OPPOSITE: White dominates my apartment but pattern defines it. The gold marbled wallpaper adds a glamorous organic touch, while the carpet brings line and detail. Even the lacquered entrance wall at right features its own three-dimensional pattern, while Andy Warhol flower prints deliver bold blocks of color.

round tables. By using the furniture to mirror the interior architecture, I could emphasize the curved forms and thereby offset the angles.

Furniture was an important choice for this apartment. Against the backdrop of white and gold, I wanted to add an element of drama. Inspired by the strong, vibrant colors of an abstract painting by Waldemar Kolbusz on the living-room wall, I introduced a navy velvet modular sofa beneath, accessorized with cushions in gold and graphic black and white. Beside this, two beige velvet armchairs contribute to the lavish effect, their brass bases mirroring the large round brass base of the coffee table. These pieces make their own striking contribution to the range of metallics that feature throughout, while the marble top of the table continues the organic lines of the wallpaper. The result is an inviting setting with a luxe 1970s vibe and a touch of Studio 54.

Across the room, white leather dining chairs bring their own lines to the dining table, tempering its angled chrome legs with a shape that blends the geometric and the organic. And so the story of pattern builds, pairing angles and curves, white, gold and navy, neutral planes and intricate surfaces. What ties it all together is that marble-effect wall treatment and the plethora of metals popping throughout.

In the kitchen, brass cabinets punctuate the subtle gray marble surfaces and patterned terrazzo floors. In the master bedroom, the brass and chrome vintage bed by Romeo Rega is the centerpiece, its strong modern lines echoed in the side table and armchair. Connecting this room to the hues of the living area, intense navy features in an armchair and a navy and white artwork by Retna, a palette combination that resonates on a more playful level in the patterned cushions on the bed.

Works of art have always counted among my most precious possessions, and they adorn the walls of my apartment, contributing to the interplay of pattern, color and intensity. The styles on display range from abstract to op art, pop to minimal and even street art. Some pick up the hues or lines of the apartment, others defy them.

A final tableau in my apartment is the en suite bathroom walls, which showcase a different type of art, yet one that is central to my heritage. Upon a recent trip back to southern Italy, I was reawakened to the vibrancy, versatility and undeniable impact of patterned tiles. Inspired on my return, I designed this monochrome mosaic for my en suite bathroom, the repeat forms of which deliver a dynamic and optical quality to the space. After coming to embrace the aesthetic value of this medium, and incorporating it into my own home, I feel I have developed a deeper appreciation for my cultural background. Having now captured The Horizon, I've found that when it comes to pattern, the sky's the limit.

OPPOSITE: Harry Seidler's iconic Horizon apartment building is known for its spectacular harbor views and unique scalloped balconies—here, pattern is inherent in the architecture itself.

FOLLOWING PAGES: Against the white and gold tones of the wallpaper and carpet, a navy velvet sofa, inspired by the colorful abstract strokes in a painting by Waldemar Kolbusz, brings a touch of drama to the living room. The striking brass base of the coffee table from one of my furniture collections echoes the base of the beige velvet tub chairs and the metallics that feature throughout.

ABOVE: A book on my marble-topped coffee table gives a nod to one of my obsessions, accompanied by my brass accessories and a monochrome Keith Herring dish. OPPOSITE: In the dining area, the round table and coffered light setting offset the angles of the chairs and the bold, hard-edged artwork by Sydney Ball.

PREVIOUS PAGES, LEFT: In the kitchen, brass cabinets pick up the veins of the wallpaper, while gray and white terrazzo floors deliver a subtle pattern. PREVIOUS PAGES, RIGHT: Monochrome geometric tiles give a dynamic feel to my en suite bathroom, combined with the lines of fluted glass and green terrazzo floor. OPPOSITE AND ABOVE: A brass and chrome vintage bed by Romeo Rega references the metallics of my apartment in a triumph of line and form. Crisp whites accentuate the blend of gold and navy.

NAVAJO SPIRIT *infuses* SOUTHWEST STYLE

As a teenager, dreaming about a career in interior design, I used to travel the world through the television shows I watched. For me back then, America seemed so far away that I wondered if I would ever get there, but I did become hooked on 1980s American hit series such as *Dynasty* and *Dallas*. The characters and their worlds seemed larger than life, and I'll never forget the huge houses and ranches they lived in.

Thirty-odd years later, it was a special experience to find myself standing outside a vast rustic property in Oklahoma, in America's glorious Southwest, and considering its renovation. To the west of me was Colorado, where *Dynasty* was set; to the south, Texas, homeland of *Dallas*. And here I was, about to design a little drama of my own.

My clients wanted to make this place their vacation home, so they were looking to turn it into an inviting, richly layered abode that oozed comfort. They requested that the design of the house take inspiration from its location and rich history. I wanted to draw on some of the influences of Native American culture as well as reference a little of the region's pioneer past. One American designer who captures these so strongly is Ralph Lauren. His Navajo-inspired textiles and lodge-style plaids and leather furniture were the perfect beginning for the story of pattern that evolves throughout this two-story, three-bedroom house.

My clients are fond of the color gray, so we painted the timber exterior in this cool hue, which I contrasted with white for the paneled trim. The pattern created by this pairing is crisp, sharp and tailored—a bold transformation that immediately takes the building from barn-style home to something more sophisticated: a contemporary rural dwelling.

Inside, timber features strongly, with black-stained oak giving a sophisticated sheen to the floors throughout and taking on a starring role in other areas. In the kitchen, for example, it brings an elegant finish to the cabinetry, which subtly references the barn style in crossed panels on the doors. The refined lines of the oak in this home create an opulent backdrop for the abundance of patterned layers.

When designing across a substantial space, pattern can be applied to the architecture itself. Such was the case here. As the ceilings stood at ten feet high, I had plenty of wall space to play with. To break up that vast surface area, I introduced a chair rail that runs throughout the house, dividing each wall. For the lower surface, I chose paneling in gray-painted timber; for the upper, plaid wallpaper by Ralph Lauren. The chair rail connects the various spaces of the house, creating a sense of continuity via this shared stylistic feature. The flow-through from the entrance area to the formal living room is emphasized by the identical

PREVIOUS PAGE: Navajo-inspired prints and colors bring a bold energy that enriches the formal living room of this grand country house in Oklahoma.

OPPOSITE: White-paneled trim creates an engaging array of patterns that work beautifully with the gray-painted exterior. I chose this color pairing for its tailored look—the combination announces that this is a rural property like none other.

use of wallpaper and paneling in both. Other rooms feature the same layout but with different interpretations. In the master bedroom, plaid wallpaper in a larger print delivers a bold result above the timber panels, which works well with the large plaid rug and stately timber bed.

For the house's white ceilings, I took a similar approach to the walls, introducing a picture rail then painting one charcoal band along the cornice and another above the wallpaper. These strong, clean lines define each room, helping to visually rein in their ample proportions and reduce the high ceilings to a more comfortably livable scale.

In the formal living room, the effect of all elements working together is powerfully evident. The bands of cornice and picture rails reflect the frames of the windows and paintings, while echoing the tones of the stained oak paneling. Introducing another level of texture to the room, I designed a wall feature for the fireplace using New York bluestone, which invests the space with an earthy character. A richly patterned rug offers another layer of warmth, visually and physically. Completing the vignette, the patterns of the furniture and blinds draw on the tones of the rug and the spirit of the house. One evokes Native American motifs, the other country lodge style—together with the paneling and wallpaper, they create a mood of modern pioneer comfort.

If the formal lounge room speaks of tailored lines and balanced pieces, the family room is more relaxed. The brief for this area was to create a lodge- or cabin-like feel for the ultimate chill-out zone. The black-stained oak vaulted ceilings already brought personality to the space. I added beams to break up the expanses of angled ceiling and underscore the archetypal pitch of the barn-style roof. As elsewhere, leather furniture, plaid upholstery and Navajo-style patterned rugs feature, but less structured wall decorations, a broader range of soft furnishings and a lower furniture profile keep the atmosphere casual.

The fact that this room connects to an outdoor living area supports its laid-back atmosphere. The vaulted roofs outside and hard-wearing timber furniture maintain the flow from interior to exterior, while blankets and cushions in more graphic prints anchor the space within its wider setting.

For me, that setting and its history make their presence known all through this beautiful home. Here, Native American-inspired patterns and lodge-style furnishings combine to create a retreat that speaks strongly of its location. Against the black-stained timber and charcoal paneling, pattern and color intertwine in a dialogue of repetition and reinterpretation, old-world layers and new-world luxury, which combine to tell a unique story.

OPPOSITE: A chair rail breaks up the vast wall surfaces throughout, allowing for a rich blend of decorative touches. The lower surface is paneled in gray-painted timber and the upper features plaid wallpaper by Ralph Lauren. Against that, a collection of old and new ornaments enhances the home's eclectic country lodge feel.

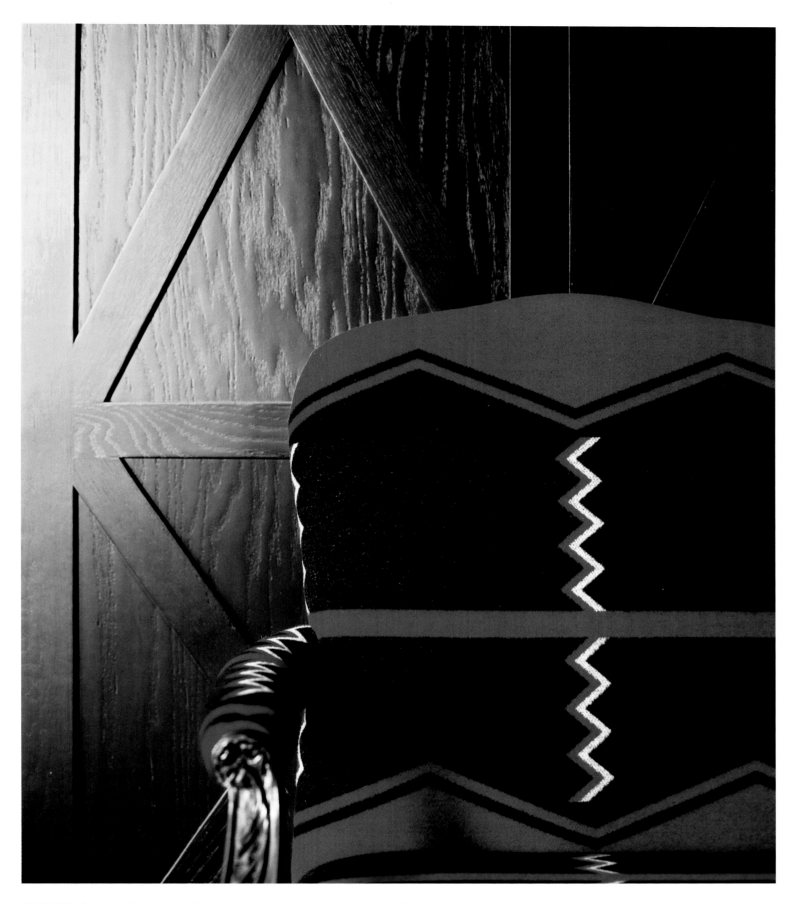

OPPOSITE: Anchored by a wall of New York bluestone, the layering of different plaids and Navajo motifs, wood, leather and hand-woven fabrics creates a vibrant and inviting setting in the formal living room. *ABOVE:* Pattern and color vibrate against the dark timber paneling.

ABOVE: Accessories great and small deliver surprising touches of detail and interest. *OPPOSITE:* Black surfaces needn't mean plain surfaces. In the kitchen, black-stained oak cabinetry brings its own pattern via barn-style paneling, while black-glazed subway tiles add a different dynamic. Beneath the sleek black dining setting, a Navajo-style cream rug echoes the expanse of white ceiling to balance the space.

OPPOSITE: The master bedroom features the same chair rail dividing timber paneling and plaid wallpaper, although here the pattern of the wallpaper is bigger and bolder. What makes it work, together with the rug in a different plaid, is the dark hues of timber and bed, which tie the look together. ABOVE: A tan leather armchair offers a moment of repose in the hallway, framed by pieces that reference the location's heritage. Different patterned rugs build up the layers of detail and color that make this house such a sumptuous retreat.

ABOVE: An example of monochromes made vivid by different treatments, this black-based bathroom reveals a range of patterns, from the inherent lines of the black-stained oak vanity and gray-glazed subway wall tiles to the more decorative layers of the floor tiles, bold red rug and striped towels. OPPOSITE: Plaid, stripes and prints contribute to the cosy mood in one of the children's bedrooms.

PREVIOUS PAGES, LEFT: An upstairs dining nook presents an appealing picture against the striking long lines of the black-stained oak vaulted ceilings. PREVIOUS PAGES, RIGHT: A detail from the family room showcases how different fabrics and finishes combine for a dynamic effect.

LEFT: I added beams to break up the ceilings and highlight the traditional pitch of the barn-style roof. The effect in this family room is cocooning and relaxed, with plenty of furniture and a mix of prints and patterns all combining to create a laid-back, cabin-like ambience.

FOLLOWING PAGES: Connected to the family room is the outdoor living area, with its hard-wearing furniture and vibrant fabrics. Here, the roof emphasizes the ample light flowing in and the wide, open access to the remarkable countryside.

ELEGANT STROKES *on a* HARBOR CANVAS

P
attern doesn't always have to be about the bold gesture and the grand statement. Subtle, textural treatments interspersed with the occasional element of surprise can deliver just as much impact. This was the case with an impressive four-story residence I designed for a couple in the smart Sydney harborside suburb of Neutral Bay. Here, pattern was an integral part of the interior design, but its role was more of a supportive one, allowing the focus to fall upon two visual wonders that the place enjoyed. The first was a treasured work of art, a large painting by the legendary late Australian artist Sidney Nolan from his "Ned Kelly" series. The second, just as much a work of art although it graces a different canvas, was the expansive view of Sydney's beautiful harbor, visible through the floor-to-ceiling windows at every level of the house.

My challenge was to design a grand yet livable space that took inspiration from the hues of the Nolan painting yet didn't fight with the vista. With a notorious Australian bushranger on one side and the magnificent Sydney Opera House on the other, the interior design needed to hold its own in such iconic company without providing a distraction.

The owners wanted a light-filled house with an abundance of white surfaces and clean, modern lines that would allow for a relaxed flow between areas. The place began as one part of a duplex, which we connected to its neighbor after knocking out the dividing wall and replacing it with a series of structural pillars. The resulting five-bedroom house is a celebration of space and natural light, and I wanted to use every opportunity to maximize both as well as emphasize those views.

A backdrop of all-white walls was an obvious choice here, but to break up the expanses of white I introduced pattern at a subtle level with white-on-white patterned wallpaper. In the main living area, the wallpaper contains horizontal lines so light they form a textural effect. In the master bedroom, it incorporates a geometric pattern that works with the details of a taupe and beige carpet to add soft tonal layers.

Other treatments of white deliver their own varieties of texture and finish, such as the gentle vertical ripples in the sheer white curtains and the giant slabs of marble in the kitchen and bathrooms. In the entertainment area, which spills out onto the sun-kissed lawn, white becomes a dazzling feature itself in a backlit white onyx bar. To add warmth to the whites, I introduced wide oak floors and a travertine staircase and feature wall. Their honey tones bring a little Sydney sunshine indoors, while their inherent patterns add depth and movement.

With Sidney Nolan's painting as the inspiration for the palette throughout, I layered the artwork's tones of plum, purple, violet and

PREVIOUS PAGE: A lilac checkerboard rug provides one of the few punches of color and pattern in this harborside home in Sydney's Neutral Bay, where white is the predominant tone.

OPPOSITE: The custom-made bronze front door makes a strong statement from the moment you enter the house; its intricate pattern brings a sense of drama to the expansive white walls and oak floors of the interior.

lilac onto the white backdrop. These provide exhilarating pops of color and appear in intense bursts on cushions, throws and vases or in softer translations on rugs. Two different tailor-made rugs bring their own interpretation of pattern to the house—one, a circular rug in lilac, white and purple; the other, a checkerboard effect in violet and white. The white pieces of furniture clustered around these rugs reflect and emphasize their patterns and shapes.

In the main living area, another pair of rugs makes a significant pattern statement that is big in appearance yet stylistically merges with the house's design. The two white rugs feature black lines in a modern take on a traditional Moroccan diamond rug pattern. From these spring the generous dining table and large curved sofas, forming an interplay of bold white shapes that allows the harbor's gems to shine before them.

Against the understated whites and refined concentrations of color and line, two considerable elements of the interior architecture make a strong contribution to pattern in the house. The first is the front door, a stunning custom-made creation of resin and metal with a bronze finish. The owners spend a great deal of time in Los Angeles, where they have another house, and became enamored of the trend there for statement doors. Bringing this element to their Sydney residence was a way of injecting a little Californian style to their minimalist haven. From the house's exterior, the door's cut-out design makes a majestic statement and offers a taste of the visual delights to come. Inside, the door appears to be a piece of art in itself that ties in with the attractive lines of bronze and stained timber throughout the house.

The second key architectural element is the floating travertine staircase with glass balustrade, which presents a dynamic study in pattern and line from several angles as well as maintaining the light, airy ambience. When I design for multi-story houses, I find that the unused space created by the staircase is the perfect spot to create a sexy vertical statement. With the owners keen to have a sculptural feature in the house, our visions aligned. Beside the staircase, I created a four-story travertine wall feature, with a bronze strip behind it that lights up at night. Not only does the wall add to the warm finishes that enhance the house, its geometric lines also reveal a striking pattern of their own.

Because both of these architectural features made such strong visual statements, and the iconic artwork and harbor views captured the eye at every turn, it was essential that the interior design for this house remain subtle. The variations on white, considered pops of color and gentle plays on line throughout show that pattern can be just as effective when it's understated.

OPPOSITE: In the main living area, pattern play is at a subtle level. A white rug with narrow black lines offers a loose geometric design, while being offset by the curves of a semicircular sofa and pair of round coffee tables. Cushions and accessories bring small variations of print and color.

The same rug, a modern version of a
Moroccan diamond pattern, appears
in the adjoining dining area. Its lines are
echoed in the pendant light and chair legs,
and juxtaposed by two stunning globe-like
purple Murano glass vases. Otherwise, the
palette remains white and light, keeping
the focus on the glorious harbor views.

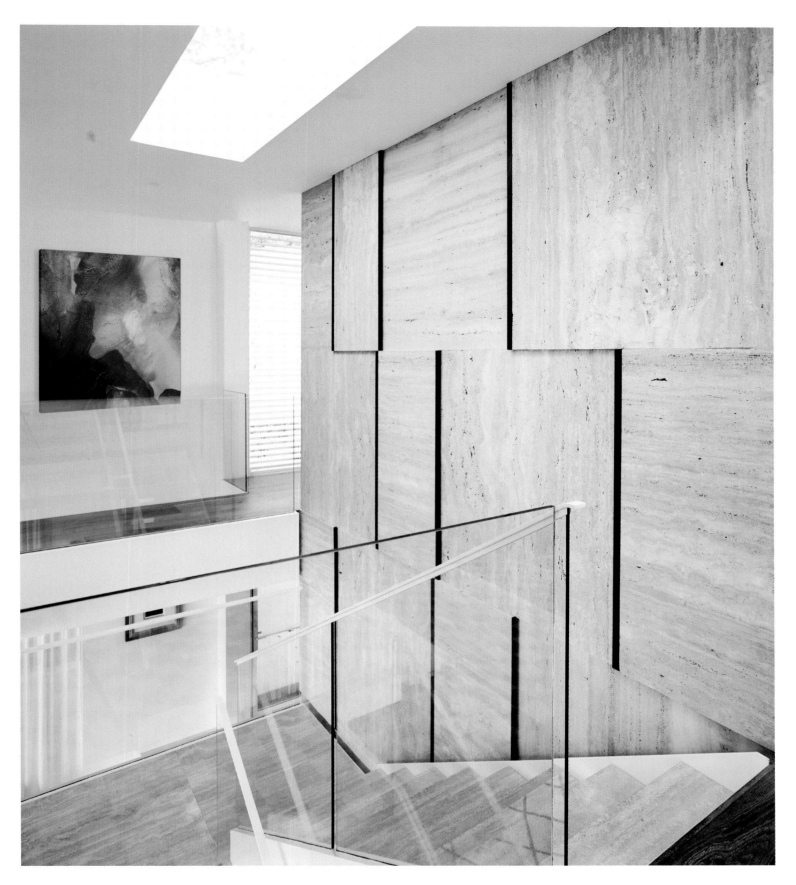

OPPOSITE: The painting of Ned Kelly by Sidney Nolan was the inspiration for the purple hues used throughout the house.
ABOVE: A key architectural element that contributes to pattern in this house is the floating travertine staircase and adjacent four-story travertine wall feature. The slabs of stone and the glass balustrade present a dynamic study in line.

A rectangular sofa and coffee table respond to the angles of the checkerboard rug in this living area, with different tones of purple in the cushions providing color and detail. Sheer white curtains bring their own delicate pattern and connect the interior to its beautiful surroundings.

OPPOSITE: The golden tones of the throw, cushions and my taupe and white geometric-patterned Yves carpet add warmth to the bedroom, where a Marilyn print by Andy Warhol brings a bold monochrome punch. ABOVE: Giant marble slabs in the en suite bathroom provide subtle details amid the luxe finishes. FOLLOWING PAGES: A spectacular backlit white onyx bar adorns the entertainment area, where the lines of the shelves, walls and furniture create an attractive interplay against the neutral tones.

OPPOSITE: Another living area where the form of furniture follows the pattern of furnishings. The curved sofa, circular coffee table and rug create a cohesive picture, their connection reinforced by the purple tones of the cushions and rug. A pair of paintings by Indigenous artist Biddee Baadjo brings strength and contrast. ABOVE: The smallest vignette can make a big impact. Here, the other-worldly swirls of a painting by Scott Petrie bring the objects in front, particular the angular lamp base, into sharp relief.

LIGHT COURTS DARK *with* GRAPHIC IMPACT

This is a tale of two city apartments, identical in layout yet a world apart in style, and it illustrates the wonderful possibilities of pattern. My clients were two friends who had bought homes in the same building in the trendy inner-west suburb of Erskineville, Sydney. Both had purchased their two-bedroom apartments at the same time, both were keen to redecorate, but the similarities ended there.

The first owner likes to wear prints and graphics, which I drew on as inspiration for the design. He wanted a light-driven ambience with strong graphic features, incorporating an interplay of black and white, with inlays of burgundy and claret tones to echo the rose-gold fittings that were already in his apartment. The second is a devotee of the color black—his wardrobe embraces it and he loves being surrounded by it. He requested a strong, sexy, sophisticated apartment that celebrated the moody tone and embellished it with warm gold touches.

So where to begin? In applying pattern to an interior, the walls are usually the initial layer I address, as they set the scene for what follows. Opting for all-white walls, admittedly a versatile backdrop in many spaces, would have resulted in too stark a setting for the first apartment. To establish a dynamic meeting and mixing of opposites, wallpaper was the answer here. Inspired by the owner's love of graphics, I introduced bold wallpaper in irregular lines, which delivers that standout factor and creates a sort of "tamed street art" vibe. The patterned walls generate light and movement, and the furnishings follow from that.

A specially commissioned painting by Australian artist Scott Petrie draws together the dark tones of the apartment and celebrates the rich reds that appear throughout. At the same time, it throws into contrast the vibrant pattern of the wallpaper and allows the white background to reflect the natural light that fills this space.

Across the hall, the dark walls make a very different statement. I wanted to reflect my client's sense of style across this vast canvas. Wallpaper is stunning but its details can dominate; paneling creates instant lines but can suggest a more classic look. I opted for hand-crafted stucco, which evokes the spirit of a 1970s sexy bachelor pad. Its pattern comes from its texture, a velvety, polished finish that transforms dramatically with the changing light. When it came to choosing the stucco's hue, black would have been too dark for this space, which is modest in size, so I opted for charcoal, which gives the walls an elegant look, against which black pieces of furniture come into their own.

This apartment also receives a healthy dose of drama thanks to another commissioned painting. In this case, the artwork, by Australian

PREVIOUS PAGE: The claret and ivory arcs of my Rio rug work beautifully with the curves of the Arne Jacobsen Swan chair and Alessi side table in this apartment in the inner-west Sydney suburb of Erskineville.

OPPOSITE: White dining chairs and a white sculpture by Dion Horstmans complement the lines of the wallpaper, with the pendant light, mirror and table delivering contrasting curves.

abstract expressionist Kerry Armstrong, provides dramatic contrast while anchoring the palette. Its white background offers some visual relief and divergence; its bold black brushstrokes serve as a stunning reminder that black is undoubtedly the star of this space.

In the living room of the graphic-based apartment, a black and white checked sofa with burgundy cushions draws its color from the painting above. The staccato lines of the walls are juxtaposed by a claret and ivory rug, the curves of which are echoed in vintage pieces of furniture such as a Noguchi coffee table and Arne Jacobsen Swan chairs. In the dining area beyond, this study in curves continues with the white chairs and circular dining table, highlighted by a round rose-gold mirror and a charismatic pendant light by Bertrand Balas.

Curves and lines play through this space, with a white sculpture by Australian artist Dion Horstmans reflecting, tonally inverting and emphasizing the pattern of the wallpaper, giving it a new luminescence.

The wallpaper takes on a different frequency in the main bedroom due to the softening effect of pale gray furnishings and sheer curtains. Here, the origami-style angles of a painting by local artist Zac Koukoravas introduce a new level of pattern that plays with the wallpaper while establishing its own story as well.

In the black apartment, the furnishings echo the moody tone established by the walls, with a black leather sofa and black upholstered armchairs in the living room, black leather-upholstered dining chairs and black-on-black décor in the bedrooms. To contrast this, I introduced tones of gold, taupe and mustard offset by white in the cushions, throws and rugs and even ceiling wallpaper. Patterned in punchy graphics and geometrics or looser, more generous organic shapes, these furnishings deliver another layer of detail and interest while softening the mix.

Gold and brass take on a glamorous edge in key pieces of furniture such as the base of a vintage Paul Evans coffee table, the cylindrical gold side tables and the gleaming ranks of brass-backed dining chairs. In the master bedroom, a vintage geometric gold and black mirror acts almost as an artwork, making a strong pairing with the side tables and Murano glass lamps. The metallics of these pieces bring their own persuasive lines of pattern to the interior design, reaching their greatest statement in two pieces. A vintage Gaetano Sciolari pendant light in unfurling gold strips delivers a burst of brilliance to the dining area, while a bespoke sideboard in gold and black panes brings the whole palette together.

A vibrant mix of black and white graphics; a sophisticated symphony in black and gold . . . These two differently styled apartments reveal how pattern can be used to enhance the mood of a place.

OPPOSITE: In the living room, graphic wallpaper keeps the focus on white and uses black for decorative touches. A painting by Australian artist Scott Petrie emphasizes the black and rich red tones that are used throughout.

ABOVE: Rounded rose gold accessories add warmth and contrast the graphics, while a cleverly placed mirror reveals new takes on existing patterns. *OPPOSITE:* A painting by Zac Koukoravas introduces another layer of pattern, softened by the gray tones of the bed. Cushions offer another small play on line, while the lamp base brings a luxe metallic touch.

OPPOSITE: Another apartment in the same block is a study in sultry black and gold. In the living room, the black tones are softened by a patterned gold rug, cushions, and the marbled look of the wallpaper on the ceiling. A painting by Australian abstract expressionist Kerry Armstrong brings contrast through its white background as well as reinforcing the sense of drama in the room with its bold black strokes. ABOVE: The gleaming metallic lines of the dining chairs and pendant light, juxtaposed by the curves of a side table, make a striking statement against the black stucco walls.

ABOVE: A standout bespoke sideboard in black and gold draws on the apartment's palette in a celebration of pattern that combines to great effect with the sculpture and lamps that sit above it. OPPOSITE: The mix continues in the master bedroom, with the geometrics of the vintage Verner Panton mirror offset by the loose organic swirls of my Ink rug. Against the gold, the different textures of black, in the walls, lampshade, bed and furnishings, ensure that it remains a strong stylistic force in this room.

RELAXED LUXURY AGAINST *a* BEACHY BACKDROP

I have always loved plaid. Growing up in the 1970s and 1980s, I remember watching Vivienne Westwood rock the fashion world with her punk-inspired plaid creations. In more recent years, I witnessed with interest the fabric's rebellious reinvention under designer Alexander McQueen and its next-generation makeover with luxury label Burberry. And observing the way David Nightingale Hicks incorporated plaid into his richly layered interior designs made a great impression on me as I was learning my craft.

From the moment I commenced the design for this sprawling estate in the New South Wales town of Avoca, I knew that plaid would feature. Not, however, the much-used red and black or camel varieties—I wanted blue. And a bright blue, at that. Avoca is a popular beach vacation destination on Australia's sunny Central Coast, and the intense blues of sky and sea are permanent fixtures here. Of course, blue plaid is nothing new. Back in the 1960s, iconic American rock group The Beach Boys famously dressed in blue plaid Pendleton shirts, ensuring that this memorable fabric would forever enjoy an association with surf and sun.

A classic beach vibe was important to my clients, a couple with two grown-up sons who wanted a traditional retreat that was both polished and relaxed. The two-story, five-bedroom house we built sits on a large bushland property just three miles from the beach, so I intended to marry country and coastal styles in its design.

In terms of palette, white was essential to create a light, crisp character, paired with blue for a chic seaside vibe. When it came to selecting the shade of blue, despite the fact that navy is a stylish color often favored for interiors, I wanted something brighter and more playful here, as befits the house's purpose and its setting. Inspired by the vivid cobalt blue of the nearby Pacific Ocean, I chose that hue for the large double doors of this residence . . . and the plaid followed suit.

That brilliant blue, translated into different patterns and a variety of intensities, is the heart and soul of this house. Behind the striking double doors, a large blue plaid rug beckons all inside, its squares echoed above in the panels of the white ceiling. Countering these right angles are a round console table and a series of circular pendant lights; beyond them a curved armchair in a shot of intense blue and another blue rug dissect the white hallway, drawing the eye further within. The picture is one of symmetry and balance, bold shapes and neutral planes, with pattern its defining frame.

Creating a classic house meant incorporating a good deal of molding into its interior architecture, which in turn allowed me to introduce a range of patterns to the walls and ceilings. Cornices, architraves, skirting and chair

PREVIOUS PAGE: A golden Theodore Alexander side table and vintage French ceramic tiled coffee table present a stunning picture of arcs above the bold squares of the blue and gold plaid carpet in this large estate in the New South Wales coastal town of Avoca.

OPPOSITE: The eye-catching rug that commands attention in the entrance makes it clear that blue plaid is a defining factor of this house's pattern story. The grid panels of the white ceiling echo the rug's details, while a series of circles in the pendant lights and console table offsets the angles. With the cobalt doors signaling the hero color within, the tone is set for vivid blues paired with crisp whites.

and picture rails are regular features, with paneling appearing throughout the house. In the kitchen, cross patterns on the cabinetry bring a beautiful layer of interest, taking the lines of the white horizontal ceiling panels and perpendicular beams one intricate step further. In the billiard room, the same ceiling panels appear in a shade of gray that evokes a sophisticated clubhouse feel.

In the main living area, the possibilities of pattern showcased in this house reach their greatest expression. Having built high roofs, I had a great opportunity to create vaulted ceilings that became a dramatic part of the home's pattern story. In this room I left the steel rafters exposed and clad them in timber, painted white to match the walls and ceiling. The attractive rows of triangular beams break up the vast space and bring the roof visually closer to the floor, an important step in giving a livable scale to such a large room. The bronze T-shaped brackets that brace the cladding of the trusses don't just serve a functional purpose pleasantly, they also have a decorative effect. Their lines are echoed in the bronze curtain rails and juxtaposed by the circular pendant lights. An enormous blue plaid rug brings color, warmth and energy, its squares referenced in the expanse of integrated wall shelving. Furniture delivers its own lines and curves, supporting the palette in tan and white. Here, pattern sings and surrounds, not only with the careful selection of each piece and its finish contributing to the rustic character of the house, but also imbuing it with a contemporary edge.

The staircase offers another enticing moment of pattern play, and another example of a functional space being elevated to remarkable by its treatment. The palette of this area may be entirely white, but it presents a fascinating study in different details. Against the square wall paneling, Chinese Chippendale design brings an openness and light-hearted complexity to the balustrade. Black-stained oak hand rails mimic the dark tones of bronze used through the house, while studded wallpaper brings an entirely new and exciting layer of pattern and texture. Central to this setting is a bold blue striped runner, which lends a pop of color and decorative interest, as well as providing a softening element against the sandstone flooring and millwork.

That lively blue, in stripes and plaid, recurs throughout the design in runners, rugs, blinds and curtains, punctuated and highlighted by blocks of blue in other pieces. The expansive surfaces of the billiard table and the lower kitchen cabinetry, for example, both deliver concentrated shots of the hue. In one of the bedrooms, a blue bed presents another solid mass of color, while the shade is diffused in various patterns around it. Blue and white soft furnishings emphasize

OPPOSITE: The entrance features many vignettes that play upon the house's central palette and pattern. Here, a painting by Scott Petrie, which features the hues of sand, sea and sky so common to this beach location, sits gracefully above the plaid rug and an arrangement of furniture that, although pared back, still incorporates the color blue.

the palette, with the wallpaper displaying a stripe in a softer tone. I have also used wallpaper on the ceilings of the bedrooms to introduce another dynamic layer of pattern. In the room with the blue bed, eye-catching wallpaper in blue and gold brings a dramatic finish to the space. In the master bedroom, where the blues are more muted and the walls feature a subtle grasscloth wallpaper, I chose a lighter pattern in metallic lines for the ceiling. To have used wallpaper across the entire ceiling would have been too overwhelming—in these large spaces, I opted for a panel of wallpaper that is framed and contained by the fresh white of the ceiling and walls above the picture rails. The result maintains the house's classic appeal and keeps the spaces light and inviting.

Blue is given another avenue to shine thanks to a diverse use of tiles throughout. I have come to love the role tiles can play in interior design. Tiles are dynamic, versatile and bring life to any space with their patterns, whether elaborate or simple. In the master en suite bathroom, my blue and white geometric tiles give a dynamic quality to the floor when balanced by white subway tiles on the walls. In another en suite bathroom, shimmering blue fish-scale tiles adorn the walls, while gray Carrara marble floors soften the effect, allowing the tiles to play hero.

The kitchen features an entirely different type of tile, a decorative Mediterranean style in the backsplash that transforms the space and gives it an intimate, welcoming feel. The warm, mustardy orange tones of the tiles work beautifully with the brass and bronze range hood, an everyday piece given a surprisingly glamorous finish, and provide dramatic contrast to the planes of blue cabinetry and white paneling. They also provide a stylistic link to the tan leather of the banquette that features in the adjoining breakout dining area.

An advantage of tiles is their power to transform and connect interior and exterior spaces, a quality particularly valuable in this house, where several areas enjoy a special link to the outdoors. In the sun room, a recreation area outside the kitchen that looks out to the natural bushland and landscaped gardens beyond, pretty blue, gray and white geometric floor tiles set the scene for a space that brings a little bit of the Mediterranean to the East Australian coast. On a verandah that runs outside all the bedrooms, those same tiles reinforce the transition between indoors and out, stylistically linking the two.

These tiles are a wonderful component of the story of pattern in this house, but for me the interior design remains all about the plaid. Just as the music of those Beach Boys in blue always conjures up images of endless summer, I like to think that the vibrant pattern brings its own good vibrations to this classic family holiday house.

OPPOSITE: The staircase showcases the role that architectural elements can play in bringing pattern to the design of a house. The light, playful lines of the Chinese Chippendale balustrade stand out against the paneling behind, with the blue striped runner and black-stained oak hand rail delivering stronger tones. Studded wallpaper adds another surprising, textural layer of pattern to the setting.

PREVIOUS PAGES: The main living area is a triumph of pattern and line, presided over by the exposed rafters. Painted in white, with their bronze T-shaped brackets revealed, the triangular series of beams creates an unforgettable profile in this generous space. OPPOSITE: A lacquered cabinet and specially commissioned painting by Australian artist Kerry Armstrong soak up and radiate the house's intense blues. ABOVE: Metallic accessories add warm luxe touches throughout the house, reflecting the golden tones of soft furnishings.

ABOVE: The long, elegant lines of a 1940's vintage Japanese chair create a strong silhouette against the crisp white paneling. *OPPOSITE:* Cobalt blue lacquered oak cabinetry in the kitchen offers another rich hit of the house's hero tone, while decorative Mediterranean tiles in deep blue, mustard and white add intricacy and intimacy. The brass range hood with its bronze trim introduces an unexpected pop of metallic.

OPPOSITE: In the breakout dining area off the kitchen, a tan leather banquette picks up the warm tones from the pretty backsplash tiles. Behind, white surfaces show that a single tone can be anything but simple, with paneling in the ceiling and barn-style cabinetry displaying a fascinating composition of lines. ABOVE: A dining setting in the house's central palette offers an enticingly detailed study in pattern.

ABOVE: Glossy subway wall tiles in the all-white laundry show how pattern and finish can transform a space. On the floor, matt hexagonal tiles add a subtle layer of detail. OPPOSITE: Rope-patterned wallpaper in the bedroom wing introduces a playful nautical theme, one of several in the house that reference its seaside location. A blue runner in another striking plaid offers colorful contrast.

OPPOSITE: In the master bedroom, grassweave wallpaper draws together the various blues of the bed furnishings, lightly patterned rug and paintings by Scott Petrie. Metallic wallpaper on the ceiling introduces another layer of interest. *ABOVE:* The pairing of blue and white takes on a softer look in a breakout area of the bedroom, where delicately patterned cushions echo the abundance of foliage in view.

PREVIOUS PAGES, LEFT: The dressing room features the same ceiling wallpaper and rug as the master bedroom, stylistically linking the two spaces. PREVIOUS PAGES, RIGHT: Geometric floor tiles add a dynamic punch of color to the en suite bathroom, with white subway wall tiles keeping the space light and bright. OPPOSITE: Another bedroom brings the deeper range of blue furnishings to a dramatic climax in a panel of stunning blue and gold wallpaper on the ceiling. ABOVE: Brilliant blue fish-scale tiles are the stars of this bathroom, with lines of fluted glass adding a subtle touch.

ABOVE: In the study, paneling at the back of the bookshelves offers an unexpected layer of pattern, while the intricate print of a charcoal rug enlivens the space. *OPPOSITE:* Pattern also comes from the textural nature of the gray grassweave wallpaper, while the tan leather chairs add warmth and suggest a clubhouse library feel. The same metallic wallpaper that features on the ceiling of the master bedroom provides a fun, glamorous finish against the darker tones here, while the white shelves and walls provide balancing lighter touches.

PREVIOUS PAGES: The interior architecture plays a key role in the billiard room, with the panels and exposed beams themselves creating pattern, painted gray here for a change of pace. Soft furnishings in stripes, plaid and organics build up layers of detail and color, highlighted by a few striking visual touches such as an oversize elliptical mirror, some standout pendant lights and attractive artwork. *ABOVE:* A cushion brings an unexpected exotic element to a luxurious cane armchair in the billiard room. *OPPOSITE:* Against the vivid blue of the billiard table, black and white nautical-themed photographs lend interest to the walls and continue the theme established by the rope-patterned wallpaper.

OPPOSITE: Furnishings in the sun room create a relaxed vibe. Sandstone bricks present a textural effect that suits the outdoor setting, with patterned tiles adding a lively look. ABOVE: The same tiles cover the verandah that adjoins the bedrooms, creating a stylish transition from interior to exterior. FOLLOWING PAGES: Around the pool, cushions, towels and umbrellas continue the house's palette in sharp, chic bursts of pattern.

COASTAL COOL *on* *a* SEA OF GOLD

For many, the words "beachside apartment" may conjure up images of surfer chic and bohemian flourishes. And while this design tale does feature a surfboard or two, it doesn't follow a predictable path. After all, the beach in question is Tamarama—or Glamarama, as Sydney locals know it— and the style stakes here are high. This is where the beautiful people gather, the bronzed, the fit, the fabulous. The Australian beach may be small, with only half a mile of shoreline, but what it lacks in size it more than makes up for in attitude. This is the fiercely fashionable setting where I helped a couple realize their two different visions in one outstanding two-story penthouse.

He is a surfer who found the ideal location in which to pursue his obsession. She is a country girl who wanted to transform the minimalist white box they'd acquired into a more layered, lavish sanctuary. It was my pleasure and privilege to create for this pair and their two children a surf pad like no other.

When it comes to pattern, I believe that walls really can talk, and the walls here tell a fascinating story that begins with the color green. My first design step was always going to be replacing the cool whites of the original apartment with a more intimate wash of color, so the only challenge was where to start. My inspiration came from a much-loved painting the owners had by the late Australian artist Ray Crooke, who was known for his depictions of Pacific Islands life. The startling array of greens in his artwork, from yellow-gold to celadon to deep forest, set the stage for me to create an interplay of hues.

In painting the walls of the apartment, I chose a deliciously light shade of sea-foam green. Not only does it bring a serene elegance to the place, it also takes on a different character in the various spaces. In the sculptural lines of the Art Deco–style front door, it assumes added depth, a hint of the details to come. In the kitchen, it imbues the cabinets with a lovely sheen, while contrasting with the darker intricacies of the green-tiled backsplash. In the living room, it merges seamlessly into the background of a splendid feature wall of de Gournay wallpaper.

The hand-painted wallpaper displays a vivid scene of birds and flowers that is at once delicate and compelling. Because it shares the light, cooling green with other walls in the house, the feature wall acts almost as a mural, a beautiful piece of art in itself that springs from the apartment's tones. Here is pattern at its most extravagant—an entire scene that is also a culmination and celebration of the chosen palette.

Given such a detailed backdrop, it was necessary to provide balance with larger planes of single tones. The camel-hued leather of a

PREVIOUS PAGE: Curves abound in the living room of this apartment in the glamorous Sydney beachside suburb of Tamarama. Here, gilt touches create an opulent mix that befits its setting.

OPPOSITE: The Art Deco–style front door is painted in the same serene sea-foam green that appears throughout the apartment. I took the idea for the paneling from the arches of the gold wallpaper; a feature brass door handle completes the picture.

Dorothy Draper sofa offers contrast and warmth, as does the appealing gleam of the brass-clad kitchen island bench beyond. These two pieces also serve to anchor the plentiful gold tones that I introduced to the apartment to offset and highlight the greens.

To speak of "gold tones" only touches the surface of what takes place here in terms of decorative effect, as the apartment's hues encompass everything from camel and honey to gilt and brass. These last two metallics play a role at several levels in the patterns found throughout the living room. The languid dollops of gold in the rug are reflected above in the organic curves of the sofa, the round coffee table with its base of curves, the spool-like side table and the strong brass base of the dining table. Brass arcs and lines wend their way around the armchairs and dining chairs, both of which are upholstered in shades of green that tie them back to the overall palette. Accessories reinforce the duet of colors, while the incorporation of mid-century furniture brings a cool vintage element that speaks of refinement and retro panache.

Gold hues form a trio of finishes from the moment you enter the apartment. Arch-patterned wallpaper picks up the tone of the travertine floors, the one featuring curves, the other long, honey-warm lines. Alongside these, sheer gold curtains seem to capture the essence of the sunlight they bring into the place. Together, these treatments lure you into the heart of the apartment, where green and gold find their forum.

The marriage of colors reaches a spectacular statement in the master bedroom, where another wall treatment speaks volumes. Not only did Ray Crooke's painting provide palette inspiration, it also suggested an enticing theme that has its roots in the 1960s vibe of his island artworks. In the rooms of retreat, I wanted to create a plantation interior style with a fashionable edge. For the wallpaper, I chose the iconic banana leaf pattern that has long been a feature of the Beverly Hills Hotel. Lush and exuberant, it embraces the tropical mood and brings another layer of pattern into the apartment. I kept the furniture neutral in tone to balance the pattern, while the brass lines of the four-poster bed link to the handsome metallic details throughout the space.

Another tropical-themed painting sits in the master bedroom, while Crooke's found its home in the reading room. It shares the space with one of several surfboards that appear in the apartment, an oversized cane chair, and a gorgeous brass daybed and coffee table. To me, that mix captures the mood of the place, where island time nostalgia gets a modern makeover via ultra-glam styling that suggests summer all year long. If the Elvis of *Blue Hawaii* fame ever needed a place to crash, I believe he couldn't have helped falling in love with this beachside beauty.

OPPOSITE: A painting by late Australian artist Ray Crooke, known for his portraits of Pacific Island life, inspired the array of greens that grace this apartment. With a surfboard and a cane chair on either side and metallics in between, this reading room merges surfer cool with city style.

The brass-clad kitchen island offers a bold gleam against the green walls, backsplash and upholstery. Its metallic finish is echoed in the pendant lights, tables and Milo Baughman armchairs; line reinforces form and color for maximum impact. The de Gournay feature wall (at left and seen in full overleaf) brings an exquisite delicacy of pattern to the space.

OPPOSITE: Against the backdrop of the glorious hand-painted de Gournay wallpaper, a camel-hued Dorothy Draper sofa sets the tone for the living room's study in curves, reinforced by the round vintage coffee table from Conley & Co and the organic pattern of my Ink rug. *ABOVE:* The dining setting follows suit with the stricking metallic arcs of the chairs, tables and lights.

ABOVE: The gilt arches of the patterned wallpaper, combined with the travertine floors and globe-like lights, create an enticingly warm entrance. *OPPOSITE:* My Malichite rug in the entertainment room features another range of greens, their swirls anchored by the brass circles of the coffee table. *FOLLOWING PAGES, LEFT:* In the master bedroom, the lush greens of the wallpaper sing, balanced by neutral tones and enhanced by the brass lines of the four-poster bed. *FOLLOWING PAGES, RIGHT:* Taupe and white geometrics in the cushion and carpet provide another layer of pattern and detail.

POPS of COLOR with a DARING EDGE

E very shade of blue you can incorporate. A variety of pattern and color welcome. Tiles a must—in fact, different tiles in every bathroom!" This was the enticingly open-ended brief I received from an old school friend, for whom I renovated and designed a home in inner Sydney. Working on this house provided me with a wonderful opportunity to integrate pattern and color throughout every surface.

From the moment you enter this one-story, four-bedroom Edwardian-era house, it reveals itself in a myriad of blues. The entrance hall features painted walls in gray-blue framed by white skirting and ceilings, and complemented by gray-stained oak floors. Those floors provide a classic array of lines, upon which I layered extra detail through the use of runners and rugs. The irregular geometry of the entrance hall runner subtly echoes the panels of the front door, its shapes and hues picked up in the paintings on either side. It's a vignette that sets the tone for the place—pattern speaks to pattern and color to color, with surfaces interacting for maximum impact.

Another hallway in the house boasts a runner of brightly hued squares, juxtaposed on the walls by the organic shapes of big, bold flowers in a series of colorful Andy Warhol prints. Here, the patterns contrast rather than complement, yet both hallways share the fine work of ceiling molding. This second hallway is one of the added features of the renovation, while the entrance hall is original, but the same ceiling treatments establish consistency between old and new spaces.

It's a strong example of pattern in the interior architecture being used to ensure a cohesive link throughout a house. A couple of the bedroom ceilings are also original, otherwise the spaces are new, but the colored walls and attractive molding are common to all. In larger areas such as the kitchen and living room, the molding assumes the form of elongated panels that play to the generous zones, whereas in the bedrooms its floral designs generate a feeling of intimacy and charm.

The family bedrooms reinforce and play with the palette introduced in the halls, with vintage-inspired lights giving each its own character. In the master bedroom, where blue, black and white dominate, a taupe and white geometric-patterned carpet adds warmth and is highlighted by brass finishes. In the son's bedroom, the blue of the walls is intensified by the playful geometrics of the rug, which fragment into a range of blues, whites and grays to match the bedding. Further color and pattern are introduced through the golden tones of the cushions and the brass of the light. The pendant light in the daughter's room is an explosion of brass lines, echoed by the brass curtain rail and frame of an elongated oval mirror. This room

PREVIOUS PAGE: Bold blue geometric tiles, shown here in the main bathroom, are a feature of all the bathrooms in this inner Sydney house. Metallic touches bring a sophisticated edge.

OPPOSITE: Against the elegant white and blue palette of the entrance hall, patterns interact and connect. The rectangles of the runner echo the panels of the front door, while the stained glass window and artworks present a mix of line and color.

features the same patterned carpet as the master bedroom, but the walls are painted a soft, alluring pink.

The change of color provides a lovely element of surprise, one of several that enhance the house's appeal. Distillations of that pink appear in the study, in a blush velvet armchair and eye-catching side table. Alongside this vignette, the taupe and white carpet, blue walls and vivid bookshelf display bring further hits of pattern and color.

Blue and pink come together in the dining room, another surprising space rich in pattern and color. Anchoring the setting is a black oak table, but from this point a symphony of line and hue takes over. Twelve chairs in four different shades of blue draw their tones from the walls, bringing a sense of delicacy but also a touch of whimsy. Beneath them, a rug in multiple shades of blue displays a free-spirited pattern that resembles marbling and reflects the abstract shapes of the pink painting on one wall. Finishing the scene with a flourish of gleaming metallics are the long pendant light and pair of brass étagères. The striking angular lines of these pieces complete the intricate interplay of line and color, making this space a vibrant focal point in the house.

And then there are the bathrooms. After all that time spent taking issue with my parents' love of tiles during my teens, it was a revelation to discover the work of Italian architect and designer Gio Ponti. The exquisite series of blue and white tiles he created for the Parco dei Principi hotel in Sorrento still impress today, and I'd like to think that a little of their magic has filtered into this hemisphere, and into this vibrant family home.

There is no doubt that patterned floor tiles bring vitality to a room. Put them on a wall as well and you create an immersive, dynamic interior. I achieved this using a different set of tiles for each of the house's three bathrooms. The tiles, customized from my collections, all feature repeated geometric motifs in blue and white and all possess a three-dimensional quality that enlivens the spaces. In all three rooms I've balanced the intensity of pattern with classic white surfaces and embellished the look with metallic fittings, frames and lights. In the main bathroom and en suite bathroom, I chose white square subway tiles with blue grout for the remaining walls—the effect is light and bright while referencing the palette. In the powder room, I took it one step further and introduced wallpaper patterned with gold flecks, inspired by the Italian Memphis design movement, for a little extra glamour and another unexpected addition.

It's that surprise element pattern brings to a space that makes it so powerful. The impulsive line, the sudden glimpse of boldness, the quick hit of color—these contribute to the art of creating compelling visual moments in a home, which reward and inspire all who live there.

OPPOSITE: Matching tiles on the floor and wall of the main bathroom create a wonderfully immersive interior. The three-dimensional appearance of these bright blue tiles gives the space a compellingly dynamic quality. White surfaces elsewhere in the room balance their intensity.

OPPOSITE: The taupe and white geometric-patterned carpet gives a warm tone to the master bedroom, reinforced by the brass lines of the curtain rail, desk and intricate pendant light. *ABOVE:* In the en suite bathroom, another set of vibrant patterned tiles creates an attractive space that's full of character. The subtle lines of fluted glass have a diluting effect. *FOLLOWING PAGES, LEFT AND RIGHT:* Patterned floor coverings and standout vintage-inspired lights offer flourishes of detail against the colored walls of the children's bedrooms.

OPPOSITE: Bold statements delineate a different hallway of the house. Here, the bright squares of the runner are juxtaposed by the large, lavish, colorful flowers in a series of Andy Warhol prints. ABOVE: A surprising little play on pink in the study provides a break from the blues that dominate the house and links the space to the daughter's bedroom, which features the color on its walls.

ABOVE: The circular grouping of sofa, coffee table and rug provides a generous contrast to the angles of the ceiling panels above. OPPOSITE: Brass lines in the furniture, cabinet door handles and along the base of the cabinetry bring a little glamour to the expanses of white ceiling and gray-stained oak floor. FOLLOWING PAGES: Line, color and pattern meet to great effect in the dining room. Chairs in four different shades of blue playfully celebrate the house's palette, while the étagères and pendant light deliver a delicate study in metallics.

ABOVE: Another view of the dining room, with the unusual handles of a black timber cabinet and patterned prints introducing new shapes to the space. *OPPOSITE:* While I used white wall tiles in the other bathrooms to balance the effect of the geometric tiles, in the powder room I introduced gold-flecked wallpaper for an unexpected and exciting twist.

ACKNOWLEDGMENTS

This book owes so much to the passion, support and hard work of many people. Thank you to my team at Greg Natale Design, past and present, who contributed countless hours to producing the projects from the building stage right through to photography. Victor Wong, Matthew Reid, Beth Godbolt, Natalie Timmins, Claire Richardson, Sally Birch, Connie Condylios, Doris Sawires, Kathryn Borglund, Renee Alam, Adam Pierpoint, Grant Tryhuba, Mark Hoyland, Lisa Dingelmaier, Nic Kaiko, Lana Stariha—I couldn't have done it without you.

To my book team, thank you for your creativity and dedication: Owen Lynch for the relentless shoot schedule and overseeing the epic two-year process with me; Fiona Daniels—always so eloquent and patient—for helping me to find the right words and knowing where to let the images speak for themselves; Anna Viniero for your art direction and graphic prowess; Anson Smart and Russell Horton for capturing these spaces so beautifully; Tiana Webb-Evans for your perseverance and counsel; Daniel Melamud at Rizzoli for your unwavering trust and wisdom. Thank you also to the incomparable Martyn Lawrence Bullard.

Some of my clients preferred not to be named here, but to all of them, these projects wouldn't have been possible without your vision, trust and dedication: Filomena and Peter Morelli, Natasha and Danny Daher, Michele and Andrew Fenton, Jo and Tim Carter, Von and Bill Wavish, Colin Slattery, Anthony Semann and Troy Bettesworth, Maree Graham and John Atwill.

Thank you to my suppliers and builders: Conley & Co, The Vignette Room, Bloomingdales, Teranova Tiles, Dedece, Designer Rugs, James Said, Becker Minty, Macleay on Manning, Space Furniture, Jonathan Adler, Justin Prol, Greg McKew, Ann Adkins, Scott Petrie, Kerry Armstrong, Megan Hess, Flinders Lane Gallery, The Rug Company, Myles Baldwin, Robert Murdocca, Vince and Melissa Ciolino, Mark Mastroianni, Paul Jones, Carmelo and Liugi Ginardi, Vlad Tomasevic and Michael Tavano.

To my parents, Francesco and Michelina, my sisters and their families, thank you for always supporting me in my crazy dream, right from the beginning when I would insist on redecorating the family home as a teenager, to letting me complete your houses today.

And finally to Jason Greenhalgh, thank you for your eternal patience and understanding.

OPPOSITE: A gold tray and a collection of quirky accessories provide a playful display above the striking monochrome carpet in this Geelong house.

FOLLOWING PAGE: Geometric and organic shapes combine in this mesmerizing view of the staircase in the Geelong country house.

First published in the United States of America in 2018
by Rizzoli International Publications, Inc.
300 Park Avenue South
New York, NY 10010
www.rizzoliusa.com

Photography © 2018 Anson Smart
Credits:
pp. 8, 57: Mathias Kiss works of art © Mathias Kiss/ADAGP. Copyright Agency, 2018.
pp. 172, 172: Biddy Baadjo works of art © Biddy Baadjo/Copyright Agency, 2018.
p. 178: Isamu Noguchi works of art © The Isamu Noguchi Foundation and Garden Museum/ARS.
    Copyright Agency, 2018.
p. 225: Ray Crooke works of art © Ray Crooke/Copyright Agency, 2018.
pp. 10, 73, 124, 124, 168, 239, 244: Andy Warhol works of art © The Andy Warhol Foundation for
    the Visual Arts, Inc/ARS. Copyright Agency, 2018.

Text © 2018 Greg Natale
Foreword © 2018 Martyn Lawrence Bullard

Editor: Daniel Melamud
Design: Anna Viniero and Greg Natale
Proofreader: Stephanie Umeda
Production: Kaija Markoe

Library of Congress Control Number: 2018938406
ISBN-13: 978-0-8478-6283-2

2018 2019 2020 2021 / 10 9 8 7 6 5 4 3 2
Printed in China